PRAYER
The Mightiest Force in the World

�֎ �֎ ✖ ✖ ✖ ✖

PRAYER

THE MIGHTIEST FORCE IN THE WORLD

✖ ✖ ✖ ✖

FRANK C. LAUBACH

FLEMING H. REVELL COMPANY
WESTWOOD, NEW JERSEY

INTRODUCTION

FEW BOOKS ON prayer have caught the public eye and heart as has this one: since its first printing in 1946, popular demand has called forth edition after edition, and the end is not yet.

Perhaps it is because it is a book covering the why, how, when and where of prayer. Or because it is a layman's book, in layman language. Or because once begun, it is a book that cannot be put away until the last word is read.

But primarily it is because it is a book born in the flame and zeal of one of the great missionaries and prophetic voices of our age. Dr. Laubach has taught millions of people to read, to become literate; beyond this, he has inspired millions more to seek and find strength as well as solace in prayer; he has made them "literate," intelligent and confident in approaching God and bringing God back to men. He regards prayer as the boundless, mightiest force in our world, ready and able to accomplish *anything*.

This book, born of his rich and rare experience, is the record of his faith in prayer, his manner and method of prayer, his exultant belief that prayer not only can save the world, but will.

It is for all who pray—or who would like to pray!

The Publishers

CONTENTS

Contents

. . . More things are wrought by prayer
Than this world dreams of. Wherefore, let thy
    voice
Rise like a fountain for me night and day.
For what are men better than sheep or goats
That nourish a blind life within the brain,
  If, knowing God, they lift not hands of prayer
Both for themselves and those who call them
    friend?
For so the whole round earth is every way
Bound by gold chains about the feet of God. . . .

Tennyson

PRAYER
The Mightiest Force in the World

I

Pray for World Leaders

THE WAR ISN'T OVER

"LET'S PRAY HARD, you guys, or this ship's goin' to blow up." That American sailor in World War II told the truth about the "good ship earth," as well as about his own carrier. For our wounded world is full of holes and fires. One more global war and we shall all be destroyed. "Pray hard, you guys, or this ship's goin' to blow up."

It helped those gobs to keep cool heads, so that they did the right thing to put out the fires—their ship still floats. Prayer will do the same thing for us. We need cool heads to do the right thing—to put out the fires of hate and prejudice, if our ship earth is to survive—and prayer will quench hate, fear and panic when nothing else will do it.

We now know that V-Day did not mark the end of the war, but only the end of one early battle. That war will not be over for another twenty years. No war is won until we win the peace. Thank God for the United Nations, but that was only a first step toward peace, for the fires of hate are burning all over the world more fiercely than ever in history. The racial hatred in South Africa, or in our own South, has in it a possibility of bloodshed as hideous as the Nazi massacres of the Jews, as every wise person sees. India, China, Argentina, and all the countries of Europe are full of dynamite which could blow up the world.

We need to mobilize a new army of ten million and train them to use a weapon as powerful for peace as rocket bombs were for destruction. Other weapons converted enemies into skeletons. This weapon must convert enemies into friends. It must heal the horrid open wound which bombs have left across the face of the world. Only prayer, which releases the infinite might of God, can win this final battle for men's minds and hearts—this battle against hate, this battle for "one world."

Right praying, Jesus repeatedly declared, can remove mountains, can accomplish anything. Before this last war many people had regarded His sweeping statements as "Oriental exaggeration," or at least not true of our day. But people are changing their minds. There is a strong and widespread swing back toward faith in the might of prayer. Much of it came from battle fronts.

Probably everybody in the United States has read some of the numerous books and magazine articles by soldiers, sailors and airmen who say they saw prayer answered.

Today few educated men doubt the power of prayer. Millions of people, however, are haunted with a guilty sense that while we have pursued scientific inquiry in other directions with enormous results, we have failed to investigate and use the mighty energies which prayer can release. Especially in this the most crucial hour in all history, when we need to employ every resource there is, we are afraid that we have overlooked the greatest resource of all.

We had better not neglect prayer now! As Cordell Hull solemnly warned us, "The human race is confronted with the gravest crisis in its experience. We who are on the scene of action have to say which way it is going." We are, in fact, in a terrifying dilemma. Science has been developing missiles which travel thousands of miles an hour, and superexplosives so diabolically efficient in wholesale killings that all scientists agree with President Eisenhower that "we cannot survive a third world war." But we have never yet had *permanent peace*. That is our dilemma. We must now find and follow some straight and narrow path never before trodden. If we do not find it, we shall perish.

The way to peace is an *untrodden* path, but it is *not* unknown. It is the way Jesus gave us.

"Love thy neighbor as thyself," not in word but in deed.

Let all men spend their lives, as Jesus did, helping others.

Let strong men sacrifice their personal advantage so that all may have equal opportunities.

Jesus' way would be peace itself if we followed

19

it. But men don't want to change as radically as
. that! They are still trying to make selfish greed
work. In the peace negotiations, nations have
jostled for special privilege, and selfish business
interests have tried to grab advantages that would
be sure to make other men hate them. Senator
Vandenberg wrote before the San Francisco Conference that nations were striving for "America
first," "England first," "Russia first,"—the very
attitude which has caused all wars. Peace cannot
be permanent until we put "the whole world
first." No part of the world, whether America or
England or Russia, or any business enterprise, is
as important as the welfare of all. "Thy kingdom
come on *earth*" is not only Christian, it is the only
possible roadway to lasting peace.

We are still in the heat of a crucial battle between the way of Jesus and the way of greed.
The Allies have cut a cancer out of Italy, Germany, and Japan; but the cancer still poisons the
blood stream of the world, and will break out
again and kill us unless we get the cancer tissue
out of our system. Nobody but God can cleanse
our blood stream, and even God can remove it
only if He has full gangway. We must pray for
God's miracle or perish. For if we refuse to yield
to God, His only recourse is to sweep us off the
earth and start over.

So this is not a time for confidence, nor is it a
time for despair; it is the time to turn to God. It
is the time for humility, penitence, desperate re-

solve, rectitude, obedience to the will of God, all-out sincerity!

Everybody is important now, all of us, young and old alike, whether in public life or in private. The future of the world depends upon whether you and enough others like you pray widely enough and often enough.

A small group of men are making the plans for world peace, plus a few hundred others who can reach their ears. All the rest of us, the hundreds of millions of us are unable to offer our views. We must be silent, but we need not be helpless. For the humblest of us can pray. Millions of us ordinary people must pour an incessant white light of prayer upon our world leaders, day after day. We must lift the heads of those leaders toward God so that they will hear Him and will obey His will. Enough people praying enough will release into the human blood stream the mightiest medicine in the universe, for we shall be the channels through whom God can exert His infinite power. Prayer is to the world of human relations what white corpuscles are to the human body. If enough of us pray enough there will be permanent peace. If we do not pray, and enough like us, hell will break loose again, and we and our homes will all be sucked into the bloody maelstrom of a third world war and perish. All of us are needed to save the world from the world's mightiest enemy, which is war itself.

21

"Prayer alone will not be enough," you say. "We need right deeds." Precisely! But prayer is the door that opens our minds and the minds of our leaders to God, so that we and they may know which deeds are right. Every man who has tried both ways to work, sometimes with prayer and sometimes without it, has discovered that truth in Archbishop Trench's wonderful poem:

Lord, what a change within us one short hour
Spent in Thy presence will avail to make!
What heavy burdens from our bosoms take,
What parched grounds refresh as with a shower!
We kneel, and all around us seems to lower;
We rise, and all, the distant and the near,
Stands forth in sunny outline brave and clear.
We kneel, how weak! we rise, how full of power!
Why, therefore, should we do ourselves this wrong,
Or others, that we are not always strong,
That we are ever overborne with care,
That we should ever weak or heartless be,
Anxious or troubled, when with us is prayer,
And joy and strength and courage are with Thee!

WE NEED A RIVER, NOT A TRICKLE

"If prayers can save the world," asked a friend, "why haven't the prayers of the devout done it already?"

Because their prayers have been a trickle, when we needed a river. The world at this moment is the *resultant of the total thought forces* which have struggled for supremacy. We had these

world wars because wills all over the world have
been at cross purposes with the will of God and
with other wills. The people who were working
and planning with God were fewer than those at
cross purposes with God's will. Hundreds were
praying, when we needed hundreds of millions.
People prayed for a few minutes a week when
they should have been praying all week, all year
"without ceasing."

THE MIGHT OF MASS PRAYER

We do not "persuade God to try harder" when
we pray; it is our world leaders, our statesmen
and church men whom we persuade to try
harder. We help God when we pray. When great
numbers of us pray for leaders, a mighty invisible
spiritual force lifts our minds and eyes toward
God. His Spirit flows through our prayer to
them, and He can speak to them directly.

We can do more for the world with prayer
than if we were to walk into Whitehall, London,
or the Kremlin in Moscow, and tell those men
what to do—far more! If they listened to our
suggestions, we would probably be more or less
wrong. But what God tells them, when they
listen to Him, must be right. It is infinitely better
for world leaders to listen to God than for them
to listen to us.

Most of us will never enter the White House
and offer advice to the President. Probably he
will never have time to read our letters. But we

can give him what is far more important than advice. We can give him a lift into the presence of God, make him hungry for divine wisdom, which is the grandest thing one man ever does for another. We can visit the White House with prayer *as many times a day* as we think of it, and every such visit makes us a channel between God and the President.

THE MIGHTIEST POWER ON EARTH

This idea struck one minister like a thunderbolt:

"Man," he explained, "if this is true at all, it is the mightest truth in the universe! It means that enough of us praying *often enough* could make everybody in the whole world look up and listen to God. We could transform the world."

He was right. Prayer is the mightiest power on earth. Prayer's power has been proven many millions of times. *Enough* of us, if we prayed *enough*, *could* save the world—if we prayed *enough!*

But the clergyman, in his enthusiasm, then went too far:

"If we could get Christians to stop and pray one minute a day, they could save the world."

I do not think that would be enough. The sun could keep nothing alive shining one minute a day. Life itself is dependent on the sun's rays, yet not one ray of light in a million produces life. Not one raindrop in a million finds its way to the roots of a tree. Not a seed in a million germinates. Not a shovelful of dirt in a million turns up a diamond in Kimberley. It is said that if all the eggs of the conger eel produced eels—and if they could find food—they would fill the space from here to the sun in two years. Nature is that extravagant! A very small proportion of our written or spoken words inspire men to *deeds*. So if we should find that our prayers do not always reach those for whom they are intended, but that every prayer probably reaches *somebody somewhere*, that is all we can ask, and more! Indeed, that fact is so powerful that if we of the Christian world pray persistently, and "faint not," as Jesus commanded, we *shall* transform the world. But occasional feeble doubting prayers will get only feeble results. One minute a day will not save us!

NO EASY VICTORY

So we must guard against expecting an easy victory. Prayer is powerful, but it is not the power of a sledge hammer that crushes with one blow. It is the power of sun rays and rain drops which bless, because there are so many of them. Instead of a minute a day, we Christians must learn to flash *hundreds of instantaneous prayers* at people near and far, knowing that many prayers may show no visible results, but that at least some of them will hit their mark. When you fill a swamp with stones, a hundred loads

25

may disappear under the water before a stone appears on the surface, but all of them *are neces-sary*.

If ten million praying people in the United States stopped for a few seconds several times every day to flash a prayer at the President or our Senators, they would feel a gentle spiritual power almost lifting them out of their chairs. Let's get ten millions to try it. We might tell these leaders by post card or telegram that we are praying, and so help them tune in to God.

"But," said a friend, "would you find ten million who are willing to pray? Isn't that fantastic?"

FIVE HUNDRED MILLION PEOPLE TO MOBILIZE

We did some figuring. We did not depend upon church membership. We looked for people who really have a *reason to pray*. All who have lost their sons, those separated from their loved ones, the wives, the sweethearts of men in the armed forces, their fathers, mothers, brothers, sisters, cousins and bosom friends, every young mother with her first born in her arms and her husband gone. All these *are* looking up to God in prayer. So are the boys who have faced death. So are the boys who have been wounded and maimed for life. Those boys without eyes or arms or legs *must* pray. They will grow bitter or go stark mad if they do not feel *necessary*, if they must only look on in helpless despair.

In this praying army belong old people who

thought they were "*has beens.*" Many people whose lives were irreligious in youth turn to God as they grow old and useless and lonesome, perhaps feeling themselves a burden on society. A husband or wife dead, and the young folks married and moved away, leaving widowed mothers or fathers alone. These lonesome old people are eager to pray if they are convinced prayer will make any difference.

There are millions of other lonesome people, for example, single men and women who sleep in furnished rooms and eat in cafeterias or restaurants. There are traveling men and women who seldom become intimately acquainted with the people they meet and never speak to the throngs of strangers whom they pass on the streets. They would pray. There are laboratory workers, scientists, men and women whose tasks keep them over noisy machinery where they are really alone, even when surrounded by people, for they are unable to talk. They could pray.

There are millions of men and women who do routine work with their hands while their minds are idling. Their work prevents them from reading, but they *could* pray. What is more, when they see that their prayers are *important* to save the world, they will pray. While sewing, sweeping, cooking, washing dishes, making beds, watching their children, women *will pray*, as Brother Lawrence did in his kitchen, if they believe that their prayers will help mold the future of their children and of their children's children.

27

All these named above total more than one hundred million. All of them *could* give hours upon hours to prayer. Their minds are empty a large part of the time, their hearts are lonesome, and they yearn to feel *necessary* and to *belong*. They want to feel they are doing something really helpful to the world. They will rise to the challenge if they believe that the future of the world depends upon their prayers.

In Europe and Asia there are millions upon millions of others who have been in the horrors of hell, with lost homes, lost families, lost careers, lost hopes, who have nowhere to look save toward heaven. Four hundred million are war victims, wretched, stunned, sickened, blasted, grasping for some way, and will pray with eager desperation, if only praying will bring a different world.

But what of the active men and women whose minds "are very busy streets," people so busy they will hop, skip, and jump across these pages— if they see them at all. They are thronged by people, by problems, and by ideas. They think there is no time to pray. But they are mistaken. There are a hundred chinks of time every day in the busiest lives, and into these chinks they could shoot flash prayers for the builders of the new world. Even when surrounded by family or business associates they could flash momentary secret messages to God.

Out of this enormous reservoir of "man power" can be recruited an army of ten million. Some of them will fill a hundred chinks a day with prayer and some ten. One hundred million prayers falling upon our world leaders every day will grip these men with a sense of sacred responsibility, a divine love for humanity, and a great hunger and thirst to look up to God and receive His plan.

And when ten million of us pray for our world leaders, think what that will do to us, as well as to them. It will make us larger, more interested in the great world issues, more likely to read carefully all the facts that will enable us to pray intelligently. Thousands of ideas will come to us of ways to help our world.

PRAYERS ARE TOO SMALL

Millions upon millions have prayed through the late war that their sons, husbands, brothers would return whole. That is good, but it ought not to end there. That prayer alone is too small which ends with our near of kin, or even with our own country. "Bring my boy home alive and well. Save us from sin and danger. Bless America." This is good but too small! People need to be taught that for every prayer for their soldier boys must go a prayer that the cause for which their boys fought may be God's will for His world.

THE FUTURE IS MENACED BY SMALL MINDS

Prayer is needed now as it was never needed in all history, that leaders may become large

enough soon enough. The men planning for a
united world have been intensely patriotic *national* leaders, and their viewpoints are inevitably
warped by their love of country. They love their
own people passionately, and as a rule have preju-
dices against other peoples, and so instinctively
grasp for national advantages. A newspaperman at
the San Francisco Conference described "seventy
small nations in the world, each one hell-bent on
getting what it wants, same as the large countries."

In these past months the newspapers and radio
have told of the recrimination of politicians, the
struggle between the British and Indian leaders,
new distrust in Latin America, the daily strikes,
the endless fight between capital and labor, the
race struggles, the disputes over air supremacy,
the intrigues of international bankers—the list of
clashing selfish efforts is very long and ugly. A
shower of prayers, gentle as snow, must fall upon
these leaders in every nation to save them from
being jealous, suspicious, greedy, prejudiced, full
of resentment and hatred, and from driving bar-
gains with weaker peoples which will breed new
wars.

At the opening of the Inter-American Conference in Mexico City in 1945, a group of Christian men and women seated in the gallery prayed
for all the delegates. That conference resulted in
agreements exceeding the expectations of the most
optimistic. Prior to the San Francisco Conference,
also in 1945, the Federal Council of Churches sent

out requests for definite prayer, and groups of praying people were organized to pray during the entire conference. Problems which seemed insoluble finally found their answers.

We must pray for Congress and particularly for senators, for they have on their hands the stupendous power of ratifying or rejecting treaties. We ought to write to the senators of our own states and to our own congressmen, telling them that we are praying for them. The letters of the most obscure people are read in Washington. Elective officers pay more attention to those who vote for them than to anybody else.

We must pray for the premier of England and the House of Commons, for the leaders in Russia, for the French, for Chinese authorities and for all others who may emerge into positions of power in this rapidly changing world.

If we pray for them for ten seconds several times a day we shall be more likely to secure results than if we prayed once for half an hour. An excellent practice is to stop for ten seconds while reading the newspapers and pray for any person who is likely to affect world affairs. Suppose ten million people read their newspapers and prayed for every important person and event! If ten million ought to do this, you and I must—we must lead, so that they will follow.

Things would come right if only we would pray. There is where we are powerful. To be alarmed or plunged into despair, or to scold—all that is futile, it only makes matters worse. The world is already in a bad humor. But when we organize a prayer army, we are with a stupendous host and with God! Desperately eager people would pray if they knew that prayer can save the world. They are waiting for us to lead the way.

FANNER BEES OF PRAYER

The perfect illustration of what we need is in Glenn Clark's parable of "Fanner Bees," in his fine book on *The Lord's Prayer*.

* There arose from the bee hive a sibilant note . . . not unlike the sound of sea waves. "They are fanner bees," whispered the old bee-keeper. "It's their job to keep the hive sweet and fresh. They're standing with their heads lowered, turned toward the center of the hive. Their wings are moving so rapidly that if you saw them you would think you were looking at a fray mist. They are drawing the bad air out through one side of the entrance, while the pure air is sucked in on the other side." The old bee-keeper stepped to the hive, holding a lighted candle in his hand. Instantly the light was extinguished by the strong current. The old man said: "The fanners draw out the bad air and let in the fresh." Isn't that how people who call themselves Christians ought to act?

Then Glenn Clark says:

* Used by permission of the author.

America has all the worker bees she needs. She does not have enough fanner bees. The greatest need in America today is for Prayer. . . . Whitefield, who achieved the most wonderful results of any evangelist who ever came to this country, always took with him a little crippled man who believed in prayer. . . . His prayers, even more than Whitefield's preaching, were the cause of the wonderful results. . . . The great army of shut-ins, the old people who think their lives are completed, the great army of invalids longing for opportunity to make their lives worth while, HERE ARE THE GREATEST UNUSED RESOURCES OF AMERICA —THESE PEOPLE WHO THINK THEIR LIVES ARE OF LEAST ACCOUNT. The stones which the builders rejected, they shall become the head of the corner! If you are a shut-in, won't you join me in the greatest crusade ever undertaken in America. . . . We want to keep it humble and invisible; that of recruiting all the shut-ins . . . into a great silent army of fanner bees! An army that shall conquer the world!

That was divine prophecy! It came from heaven to Glenn Clark.

SILENCE IS MORE POWERFUL THAN NOISE

Prayer is likely to be undervalued by all but wise people because it is so silent and so secret. We are often deceived into thinking that noise is more important than silence. War sounds far more important than the noiseless growing of a crop of wheat, yet the silent wheat feeds millions, while war destroys them. Nobody but God knows how often prayers have changed the course of history. Many a man who prayed received no credit excepting in heaven. We are tempted to turn from prayer to something more noisy, like speeches or guns, because our motives are mixed. We are interested in the making of a better world, of course, but we also want people to give us credit for what we have done.

Secret prayer for others all during the day is an acid test of our unselfishness. Our little selves must fade out, leaving a self-forgetting channel, through which God's warmth flows unhindered in lovely unending prayer. The highest form of communion is not asking God for things for ourselves, but letting Him flow down through us, out over the world—in endless benediction. In the old Hebrew story Sodom needed ten good men to be saved. Now the world needs ten million. Anybody Christian enough to have read this far must be one of that ten million or there will not be enough to save our age.

II

Pray for the Church

THE WORLD cannot be saved by three men, or by five hundred around peace tables, even though their plans come out of heaven. Their work is vital, but it is not nearly enough. They draw the blue-prints of peace; but treaties become scraps of paper when men and nations hate or rankle under the sense of injustice, as four men out of five in this world are doing now. In Africa, Asia, the East Indies and Latin America the illiterate three-fifths of the human race are slaves, penniless, hungry, sick, engulfed in hopeless debts, driven to grinding toil from dawn to darkness. Three-fifths of the human race are in deeper poverty, hunger, depravity, ignorance, fear, and despair than any slum in the United States. Misery covers four-fifths of the world. In these wretched areas of hate and resentment new Hitlers will find eager ears.

Bombing these victims of despair if they attempt to revolt against the status quo will not prevent a third world war. A police force cannot keep a billion and a quarter starving victims down with tanks and bombs. They outnumber the people with plenty, five to one. To defeat them we should have to annihilate so many millions that Hitler would seem a saint by comparison with us. We would not defeat them. God was with us in the last war, but He would be on the side of the oppressed if we fought against them. It is we who would be destroyed by Him and by them. The crux of the peace problem is not the power to frighten suffering men into submission, but the power to heal their misery: this is the way of the Good Samaritan, the way of Jesus, and it is the only way out.

We must heal this festering area of misery as swiftly as possible. By 1965 we shall know whether we are headed towards permanent peace or towards another hell. We must labor with loving service, and it will require devoted men and billions of dollars, for this is a large world. Who will do it?

Can we expect our own Congress to help the world adequately? The government of the United States is in debt more than two hundred billion dollars, by far the largest debt in history. Congressmen and senators hear an insistent demand from taxpayers to ease the burden of taxation. Congress will help our Allies in white Europe and our own Philippines, but will do too little to help the chronic horrors of Asia and Africa. Yet Asia and Africa will not wait. The very fact that we help white Europe and the Filipinos and neglect the rest will produce the same resentment against our racial prejudice that rankled in the soul of Japan. If we wait ten or fifteen years a

36

third world war will breed in neglected Asia. Our vast program for the colored peoples of the world must be started immediately; our own destruction will be the price of delay. It is a *must*.

Who can do it? The people of America, they who are in a financial position to do it. Our government owes hundreds of billions to *us*. We are rich in government bonds. The more the government owes, the richer we are. One per cent of these bonds would be more than enough to save the world from want and despair.

The Christian Church of America not only has the financial resources adequate to save the world, but she has her vast missionary network all over the world. This is the arm with which the Church can reach out and rid the world of the dangerous festering areas of despair where the next wars are breeding. Missionaries are better prepared than government diplomats to meet and lift the *neediest* people. Wendell Willkie reported after his trip around the world that he found the missionaries were the most popular foreigners in every country. Our ambassadors and consuls mingle with the officials and the élite of other countries. Missionaries work in the hovels of poverty with the sick, the lepers, with the dirtiest and most illiterate. They are diplomats to the masses. They work for the love of Christ at a mere subsistence wage. In turning hatred into love, vice into virtue, and ignorance into light they can achieve more with ten dollars than governments can achieve with one hundred.

PRAYER

One section of the Foreign Missions Conference, representing sixty-two leading Protestant communions of the United States and Canada, declared at its annual meeting in January, 1945:

We realize the painful eagerness of the peoples of the world to prevent a third global war, and that we have a real and urgent responsibility as a missionary body to remove the misery, intolerance, injustice and ignorance which will inevitably bring such a calamity upon us even though governments do all they can. We believe that the missionary enterprise of the Christian Church is an instrument which, in the hands of God, may be used to cure many of the basic causes of war. By the transforming touch of Christlike service we would pursue more vigorously the superhuman task of changing despair to hope, ignorance to enlightenment, stagnation to progress, destitution to an abundant life, disease to health, and hate to love.

Again in June, 1945, the Conference approved an even stronger statement:

Thinking people [it said] are desperate. They want hope, and a Plan, something they can do instead of looking on in helpless dismay. The Church through her mission program has the only ultimate hope and it is the way of Christ.

Our plan is to send many Christ-filled missionaries with technical training to try to heal all the festering sores where the next world war is breeding. In missions alone are the machinery,

38

the spirit, and the experience for this under-taking.

Here is the plan more in detail:

1. Tell the church, tell America, tell the world. "Missions will do their best to help remove the misery, ignorance, and hate, where wars breed, and to form a friendly co-operating world. Give us the backing we need, and by God's help we shall not fail."

2. Further unify the missionary efforts of the churches. We already have a united medical program, a special leper program, a united agricultural program, a united literacy program, a united committee on rehabilitation and relief, a united committee on co-operation in Latin America, in Africa, in India, and United Christian Councils in most mission lands. Missions are more united than the home churches, and are constantly getting closer.

3. Survey the needy areas of the world, asking governments and people what help they will welcome. Say: "We have not suffered as you have, but this at least we can do in humble love. We can share our surplus with your need. We are especially eager to enable you to help yourselves."

4. Prepare a budget based upon the world's requests for help, asking for a gift of no less than a $25 bond or its equivalent from every church member—$25 up! Forty million Christians at $25 would be a billion dollars.

5. In addition to evangelistic missionaries, Christ-filled men and women with a love of people and free from racial prejudice will receive technical training so that they can go as specialists to meet definite needs.

6. More vocational schools are being geared into technical preparation for missionaries and should include courses on the customs and habits of other people.

7. Missionaries all over the world must be urged, in these next twenty fateful years, to strive for co-operation and good will, and to prevent religious or political or social controversies. They must be the *peace makers* of the world in this crisis.

8. The Church is asking all governments to co-operate with this good-will program. "Remove all red tape and obstructive legislation," it says, "and prevent selfish private enterprises from blocking or neutralizing this program; clear the gangway and let us all together lift the world out of its danger."

9. This plan does' not soft pedal evangelism. Missionaries have found that when people are in misery "deeds speak louder than words." Now the half-dead world needs to see the gospel in action. We cannot make people love Christ until we help them. Then they see Him in us.

Here is a challenge that stirs men's blood with resolve; it does not put them to sleep with the deadening notion that everything will turn out right no matter what we do. It fires them with the conviction that *we can save our country and our age by being Christian enough,* that if *we* do not do it, *NOBODY WILL.* We Americans and nobody else in this awful day *can and must* be God's instruments. To this challenge every real man and woman will rise.

THEREFORE PRAY FOR CHRISTIANS

Pray, therefore, for the Church's plan.

Pray that American Christians may become *large-visioned enough soon enough* to pour out their prayers, their money, their love, and their youth over all the world.

Pray that people with war bonds may convert them into *Peace Bonds* by giving them to Mission Boards, enough bonds to meet the emergency.

Pray that the white race may become *color blind.*

Pray for missionaries! Every missionary needs ten thousand praying backers.

"But," asked a friend, "do you think American Christians would be that idealistic, that Christian?"

Many would not, at their present low spiritual temperature—not until the Church experiences a mighty spiritual awakening. Cold Christians will not give their lives and will give little money to missions. But when Christians are full of Christ, they will give life and money until they feel the ecstasy of sacrifice. Therefore, one thing upon which the fate of the world hangs is a *pentecostal* awakening of our American churches. Prayer is the power which always turns dead churches alive, and makes small Christians big—prayer plus a tremendous sense of being needed, a gripping cause. We have the cause. We do not yet have enough prayer.

The first place for us to center our prayer is upon our own congregation, to say: "Lord, save the world and begin right with us." How, then, can we start a pentecost in our church?

WHAT HAPPENS WHEN A WHOLE CHURCH PRAYS

Some of us urge congregations to pray while we speak. "I am very sensitive," the preacher tells them, "and know whether you are praying for me. If one of you lets me down, I feel it. When you are praying for me, I feel a strange power. When EVERY person in a congregation prays intensely while the pastor is preaching, a miracle happens. If it does not happen today, somebody has failed to pray. Let us make it unanimous, and see what happens when EVERYBODY is praying."

The results of this appeal are always good, and sometimes they are marvelous. A feeling of something solid as steel comes when people become one in prayer. At a Camp Farthest Out* the

* "Camp Farthest Out" is a project founded some twenty-five years ago by the late Glenn Clark; there are thirty-nine of them, across the United States and abroad, meeting each summer to engage in prayer and faith-building activities. An average of a hundred or more of all ages attend the summer camps, and many of them meet once a month or oftener during the year to carry on their work.—Ed.

group became so trained that they prayed with great intensity and harmony. One evening while they prayed the speaker was lifted out of himself and seemed to be possessed by Christ. He felt as though Christ were talking through his lips. Many others shared his experience. Six people came to him and said, "We saw Christ standing by you."

As he went out of the church a woman was sobbing with her head on the seat. He sat down beside her and asked her if he could help her.

"I don't believe in such things," she said, "but what can I do? I saw Christ myself!"

What had happened? The audience was so melted into one by prayer that it had in some way enabled the Invisible Christ to become visible to about a dozen eyes.

A most extraordinary experience of what an audience can do to a speaker occurred at an open-air civic center in Denver. The speaker appealed to the large audience to pray while he talked.

Five hundred wounded boys at Asheville, North Carolina [he said] nearly wept when I told them they could still help by praying for world leaders. Tomorrow I am going to speak to seventeen hundred other sick soldiers at your Fitzsimmons Hospital, and many of them will weep, because they care: they are wounded! *They* will pray. But do *you*, the fathers and mothers, wives and sweethearts and friends of these wounded boys, care enough to pray like those wounded boys pray? Or don't you care that much?

43

That outraged audience struck back! Something invisible gripped the speaker's arms. Involuntarily, he grasped the table in front of him. The next moment it lay on the floor in splinters, and the microphone had been knocked over. It seemed to the speaker that he had not broken the table, but that the audience had done it. He picked up the microphone and finished his talk. That night he lay awake half the night trembling at the strange thing that that audience had done to him. A man wrote that he was converted when that table was shattered.

THE LAME WALK

Often, diseases are cured when people are united in prayer. For seven years a woman had suffered more or less in agony from a growth on the spine. The last two years she had not been able to walk, and the pain had become very acute. Mayo Hospital set a date for an appointment, but the doctors did not promise they could do anything more than possibly relieve the condition temporarily. The woman and her husband went to Wisconsin in their car all the way from West Virginia, and found they had almost two weeks before the Mayo appointment, so they went to Camp Farthest Out at Lake Koronis. From the time of her arrival, individual and group prayers were focused on her healing.

On Sunday morning Glenn Clark announced

he was going to speak on "The Sufferings of Job." The afflicted woman prayed that her pain would permit her to hear the talk, for the Book of Job was her favorite Bible reading. When the speaker came to the climax of his address, using the verse, "Though he slay me yet will I trust him," she suddenly felt a gentle hand touch the top of her head and move slowly down her spine. Where it touched the place of the acute pain, the pain vanished immediately and new life coursed through her being. She walked out of that meeting completely healed. A few hours later she was running down the road.

Healings like that are by no means infrequent where every soul present is in tune. That a large group connected by common prayer is more powerful than one man alone seems apparent.

In nearly all congregations where we plead for every listener to pray hard we feel a strange, strong, delightful response from all parts of the room. Always, when congregations pray with great earnestness and unanimity we feel lifted almost as though an invisible arm held us up; our hearts burn, tears lie close, and ideas come fresh and far better than any written address. Commonplace truth becomes incandescent, and burns like liquid metal. A congregation is three-fourths of a sermon! Pastors around the world in ever increasing numbers are testifying that their preaching has been transformed by asking people to lean forward and pray.

PRAYER

The following letter has been widely distributed to be read by Sunday-school teachers to their classes:

Dear Church Member:

We are going to form a conspiracy today, to pray while our pastor is preaching. Don't shut your eyes unless you wish to, but keep asking God to speak through the pastor's lips and in our hearts.

It will be an exciting experiment. Remember, you are the church, and the pastor is your servant. Each of you is just as important in making a great service as he is. He can't do his best alone. Your prayer sets the spiritual atmosphere without which no sermon can be great. Together we can lift the pastor and the service to new heights. Miracles happen when a congregation makes this unanimous. It will not be unanimous unless it includes *you*.

You want to help our world out of its deep trouble but you can't do it *alone*. Christ must be able to work through you to make the world safe, and bring lasting peace. Praying together in this church today is one grand way in which we help Christ to give us vision and power to lift the world.

So pray inwardly every minute, and see what happens.

HOW PENTECOSTS BEGIN

When a congregation prays in solid array, we have the same conditions as they had at Pentecost, when, the Book of Acts says, "These all continued with one accord [unanimously] in prayer and *supplication*. . . . And when the day of Pentecost was fully come, they were all with one accord in one place. . . . And they, continuing daily with one accord in the temple, and breaking bread from house to house, did eat their meat with gladness and singleness of heart." Somebody could make a wonderful study of the manifestations of the Holy Spirit in the last two thousand years of the Christian Church. He would, I think, find this statement to be true: "The Holy Spirit is ever eager to break through, but fails, except where He finds loving, joyous unity in prayer."

The first Pentecost shows us also what to expect when the Holy Spirit comes. We may expect the unexpected—perhaps outward evidences like tongues of fire, or a shaking house, or prison doors opened. But Pentecost also wrought results *in people:* "And all that believed were together, and had all things in common; And sold their possessions and goods, and parted them to all men, as every *man had need.*" Selfishness, the most common of all sins against Christ, melted into generosity. There were also results in people of the surrounding community. "The same day there were added unto them about three thousand souls." The greatest of the results of Pentecost was a spiritual explosion. Christ-filled men and women went all over the world to tell the glad news.

It has been the vogue among us educated people to look down upon the ignorant congregations among whom manifestations of the Spirit are most common. But it will do us no harm to ask ourselves (at least once in a lifetime) this question: "Do the simple people perhaps fulfill the conditions of the coming of a Pentecost better than we do? Does a Negro camp meeting have a oneness of spirit, an utter surrender, a sharing of all they possess with one another, such as we seldom achieve among all the members of a well-to-do or sophisticated congregation?"

We think these "manifestations of the Spirit" are produced by ignorance; perhaps they really depend upon surrender, faith, unity of spirit, generosity, utter penitence, and humility.

Some of us *are* seeing unexpected and marvelous visitations of the Holy Spirit among highly educated people whenever they become as humble and full of love and united into "one accord."

The effect of prayer is like genius—fresh, surprising, astounding—but safe, utterly safe! So, my fellow minister who may be reading these pages, if your cultured leaders sit back in judgment every Sunday while you preach, don't let them defeat you any longer. Teach them to stop leaning back in judgment and to lean forward in prayer. Then expect the impossible!

G. Campbell Morgan, in *The Practice of Prayer*, tells of Marianne Adlard, a bed-ridden girl in London, who read of the work of Moody among the ragged children of Chicago. She began to pray, "O Lord, send this man to our church."

In 1872 Moody took his second trip to England, not intending to do any work. But the pastor of Marianne's church met Moody and invited him to preach for him. Moody came, and after the service asked if anybody desired to decide for Christ. Hundreds rose to their feet. Moody was so surprised that he repeated his request more clearly, and they rose again. During the next ten days four hundred persons were received into the church. Moody told Morgan, "I wanted to know what this meant. I began making inquiries and never rested until I found a bed-ridden girl praying that God would bring me to that church. He had heard her, and brought me over four thousand miles of land and sea at her request."

Moody was unusually sensitive. Professor Franklin Giddings loved to tell his classes in sociology how, when he was a cub reporter, he had attended one of Moody's revival services, and had followed hundreds of others into an after meeting for prayer. Moody, suspecting his real purpose, pointed his finger at young Giddings and said, "Young man, leave this room. You are not here to pray."

MAKE PRAYER THE CLIMAX OF THE SERVICE

The Roman Catholic Church secures the united and intense prayer of all present at the moment of the elevation of the host. Protestants need to achieve a sublime climax in the prayer period as unifying and stirring as the Catholic mass. This will come only when minister and people are sure of this, *that every prayer we utter from the heart begins to change history at once.*

Most prayers of intercession one hears in church are tragic disappointments, meager, vague, half-hearted, powerless, small. People seldom pray as if they realized that *prayer changes the world.*

Evangelical Christianity is lost unless it discovers that the center and power of its divine service is prayer, not sermons; God, not the preacher. This does not mean that more time must be spent in preparing written prayers, it does mean that minister and people need to spend more time preparing themselves for the service by prayer at home. In order that they may be alone in prayer, some ministers do not have breakfast with their families on Sunday morning.

AN INNER CIRCLE OF PRAYER

A *small* group of praying people need not wait for an invitation from the pastor or for the rest of the congregation. They can band themselves together in prayer, and if they persist long enough and earnestly enough, they will set a church on fire. It is hard work, but the reward is wonderful. The commonest of all methods of bringing a dead church back to life is to form an inner prayer circle.

ONE PRAYING PERSON IN CHURCH

Even one person praying alone in a church can do a great deal toward raising the spiritual temperature. We who travel much among strangers have many opportunities to try this. Often we sit in the back of the church incognito and pray for the service. When we enter the church we may sense that the congregation is listless and the preacher is defeated by their dullness of soul. It is a hard fight to pray against such a frozen current, but the harder it is, the more it is needed. So we literally fight for God. We pray for everybody, as well as for the pastor. While we are praying with intense concentration, we feel the Holy Spirit moving the speaker; his voice takes on a new timbre, his face a new radiance. He leaves the written sermon, which becomes too cold for him, and utters inspired words which come to him.

Several years ago, in St. Petersburg, Florida, my eyes were caught by a white-haired woman, dressed all in white, with a pale, sympathetic face, and I talked, looking straight at her. She seemed to be drawing from me better than my best, and I felt inspired. At the end of the meeting she came to the platform, and I told her how she had helped me. "That was because I prayed while you talked," she said. "I know what that can do for a preacher; my husband was a minister."

One Easter morning I entered a church in Bombay, India, a total stranger, and sat in the rear pew. The sermon was hopelessly bad, and I, who had come to receive an Easter blessing, was exasperated. I said to God, "I at least will help these cheated people." I began to pray in silence at the backs of their heads, one at a time. To my astonished joy every person, almost the moment I prayed, either turned, or bowed his head, or looked toward the ceiling, or shook his head, or passed his hand over the back of his head. I have never before nor since experienced such a one-hundred percent response.

Before some of us speak in a church we close our eyes or look at a favorite picture of Christ and try to raise the spiritual temperature by praying hard for one pew and then another. We imagine Christ descending from above upon the people or walking down the aisle with tearful wistfulness, touching one after the other. It is so hard to fight the "secular" atmosphere of many churches that every nerve aches. But the effort is infinitely rewarding. One's own soul catches fire, and after nearly every such service people say, "We felt Christ," or "The Holy Spirit was powerful today."

It is more important for a preacher to have *himself* and *his congregation* ready than to have his sermon ready.

✳ III ✳

How Prayer Helps God

AN HONEST CLERGYMAN confessed that he was baffled by a problem which puzzles many people. "I do not believe that prayer for other people does them any good *unless they hear me praying,*" he said. "When I pray with my congregation before me, they hear what I say, and I open their minds toward God. That is understandable. But when I pray for a Russian leader ten thousand miles away, what happens? I surely cannot persuade God to try harder to help him, for God is like Christ, always doing His best. So what's the use?"

This is how I answered him:

"You can't escape facts. The fact is that thousands upon thousands of people are being helped by intercessory prayer even when they are beyond the range of our voices. Missionaries beg people on the other side of the world to pray hard for them. They feel power when others pray, and are weak when others stop praying. Have you seen the poem, 'The Power of Intercession'?

Away in foreign fields, they wondered how
  Their simple word had power—
At home, some Christians, two or three, had met
  To pray an hour.
We are always wondering—wondering how,
  Because we do not see
Someone—perhaps unknown and far away—
  On bended knee.

"Ten thousand people in America promised to pray for our literacy work. Their prayers have opened the doors of men's hearts around the whole world like an invisible love force, and have made impossible obstacles melt away like steel before a blow torch. The enormous results which appear when many people pray is *what makes me sure we can do any good thing if enough of us pray enough.* Intercessory prayer is as irresistible as Jesus declared it was—'Whatsoever ye ask in my name believing it shall be done.' He said that a dozen different ways.

"But you ask *why,* and the answer is not easy. You are right when you say that God always does His best, and that we do *not* persuade God to try harder. There is another explanation—that we *persuade people to listen to God.* That is what you do when you pray in front of your congregation, persuade them to pray with you and to listen to God."

"Persuade *them?* How could we, when they are far away and don't *hear* us?"

"Perhaps they *do* hear us," I told him. "Their subconscious minds *might* hear us with that sixth sense called telepathy. That is a *possible* explanation, and recent experiments make it reasonable. Every mind, it now seems probable, unconsciously receives more or less messages from other minds. We all know people who felt intuitively when their loved ones at a distance went through peril or pain or death. The British and American Annals of Psychic Research contain thousands of these instances. Recent experiments, especially those of Professor Rhine of Duke University, have silenced the majority of doubters concerning extrasensory perception.*

"Like radios, we seem to be tuned in to each other a part of the time, and turned off at other times. Our tuning-in buttons seem to be in the unconscious mind and nearly out of conscious control, just as the heart beat is nearly out of our control. It is likely that every time we think intensely, some people near and far who happen to be tuned in to us get our thoughts without knowing where their ideas come from. It is likely that we are catching other people's thoughts all day long without knowing it. A broadcasting center never knows who may be tuned in. New discoveries in electronics are being made every

---

* *Reader's Digest*, Jan., 1944. *Atlantic Monthly*, Aug., 1944. *American Magazine*, Sept., 1944. *Journal of Psychotherapy*, Duke University Books. *Mental Radio*, by Upton Sinclair. *What's on Your Mind?*, Joseph Dunninger. *Extra-Sensory Perception*, Prof. J. B. Rhine. *New Frontiers of the Mind*, The Duke University Press. *Experiments*, Professor Rhine. *Telepathy and Clairvoyance*, Professor Rhine. *Thoughts Through Space*, Sherman and Wilkins.

month. Possibly telepathy employs electronic energy as the radio does, but on the other hand telepathy may be 'pure mind' or 'purely spiritual,' for all we yet know."

"I believe in telepathy. In fact, I have experienced it. Who hasn't?" said the clergyman. "But how does telepathy help God?"

HOW WE UNLOCK THE DOOR

I replied:

"Christ says, 'Behold I stand at the door and knock.' But God cannot get in, for most men have their doors closed toward Him nearly all the time, and many have 'lost the key'; they never talk to God. People listen to each other a million times before they listen to God once. Their thoughts are turned outward, not upward. If you pray for a man a thousand miles away, his unconscious mind may at that very moment be attuned outward toward you. If so, he will get your prayer and that may start in him a desire for God. *Desire* is what tunes men in to God. If you thus help turn a man toward God, you perform the service of a telephone operator, you connect the man with God. That helps God to speak to him directly.

"Suppose, for example, a hundred people are praying for the President of the United States, 'Lord, help the President to feel hungry and thirsty for Thy wisdom,' and the President is tuned in to some or many of that hundred. If so, he will get their prayer subconsciously and will feel a desire to look up, listening to God; then God can tell the President directly the right answer to his problems.

"Thus, by praying, people help God reach the President just as you help God reach your congregation *when they hear you preach or pray in church*. The President *hears* them by mental radio."

A dozen of us had an electrifying demonstration of this at a retreat in Washington, D.C., on January 2, 1945. We feel that President Roosevelt needed our prayers because the future so greatly hinged upon his doing God's will. So we decided to send Walter Judd and Rufus Jones to see the President, but, first, we all prayed. Here is the secretary's report of what happened:

"Somebody placed a picture of President Roosevelt on the mantel beside a picture of Christ. 'Let us try to see Christ speaking to Roosevelt,' he said. After a long silence, a wonderful thing happened. I never before saw a Quaker kneel, but Rufus Jones knelt and offered a powerful prayer for Franklin Roosevelt. As this great man knelt, I saw him lifted so far above Roosevelt that I felt the very heavens pouring down through him and flooding Roosevelt with light and love and humility. In another room the phone rang, and Roosevelt's secretary, Miss Tumulty, gave a long personal message to our hostess, Marion Johnson, from her cousin, Franklin Roosevelt. When the news of that message at that moment came, Glenn Clark said, 'This was a ribbon of love between the White House and us. I know our prayer was "on the beam." ' "

"Prayer," said Walter Judd, "can reach Roosevelt through the ether better than a visit of Rufus Jones and me to him in body. Let us not attempt to give any resolutions to the President, but let the prayer alone do the job."

There is nothing unorthodox in this supposition. When telepathy is finally proven, it will be a scientific reason for being orthodox. It will mean that telepathy and answered intercessory prayer both employ a sixth sense, just as praying aloud and conversation use the vocal cords and ear drums, and just as the radio is often employed to preach through the ether.

Certainly there is nothing *ethically wrong* in telepathy. God hears our silent prayers and we hear His silent answer from mind to mind, or, in other words, telepathically. If telepathy operates between God and man it is just as right to use telepathy for drawing others to God as it is to preach to them in church. It is not a question of right or wrong. Nor is it a question of taste or distaste. It is only a question of fact. Is it a fact or isn't it?

PRAYERS ARE NEVER LOST

"But," asked a minister, "if the other man is not tuned in to me when I pray, is my prayer lost?"

"That," I replied, "is one more thing we do

not know yet. When you pray in church, what percentage of your congregation really are listening to you? You might be horrified if you knew. But even if the people we pray for are not tuned in, somebody somewhere in the world *is* tuned in and catches our prayer. Every prayer is a world broadcast, and somebody always is listening in. So your prayers are never wasted. No prayer ends with your congregation. Even if your flock are not listening, your prayer reaches an audience thousands of miles beyond the reach of your voice. It goes around the world!"

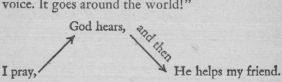

But the formula which would express *"our helping God"* is this:

My friend is closed toward God but open toward me.
By prayer for him I open toward Him and God.
Then God speaks to him through me.
My friend feels a desire for God and opens toward Him.

The diagram would be like this:

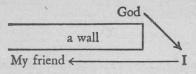

This is exactly what we do when we *talk* to our friend about God, or *preach* at him from a pulpit, or talk to him over the radio, or *write* him a letter about God, or *send* him a Bible. The same things happen when we pray, because the mind is a "mental radio." Many of us, because we believe this, pray with great faith—and when there is great faith there are great results.

This idea of *helping God* fits in perfectly with His loving nature, with man's stubborn nature, and with what the Bible tells us.

HELPING THE UNBELIEVER

A prominent Christian leader recommends leaving this idea out of this book because it might prove objectionable to some devout persons who are rooted and grounded in the other idea. On the other hand, many college teachers and students who have never prayed much for others insist that this is the most valuable contribution to the modern man's faith in the entire book. Scores have testified that it has given them a new reason to pray and a new experience of God.

So here was the choice: to risk losing either the complete endorsement of some grand old saints or those who want to believe in prayer yet have no logical basis for their faith. There can be no doubt which choice Jesus would make: "They that are whole need no physician, but they that are sick." He said, "I came not to call the righteous but sinners to repentance." There are multitudes of sinners against prayer, by their own confession. "I, a minister, don't pray," writes a man in today's mail, "and how can I teach others to pray?" There are multitudes whose prayers are wholly adoration and submission—never intercession. Here before me are three large volumes on the subject of prayer—but intercession is dismissed with a few sentences. Those who need no physician for their prayer life are very few, compared with the multitudes who are spiritually drowning and reaching for help.

This explanation is left because it is helping many troubled souls. There is no choice.

SEPARATING TELEPATHY FROM BAD COMPANY

Some people dislike associating prayer with telepathy, because telepathy has been associated in their minds with sleight-of-hand and gypsy fortune-tellers. Well, so has prayer been associated with voodoo. And so have medicine and chemistry been mixed with alchemy until recent years, and there are still some "quack doctors" to be found.

Telepathy has come into very respectable company since the invention of the radio. Some universities are studying it in parapsychology classes. Its most recent triumph is with the blind.

Scores of blind people are learning "how to see without eyes."

"Call it 'sixth sense,'" says Dr. Levine. "Call it 'human radar' or what you will. I cannot explain its mechanics—but I do know it works.

"Roughly, 'human radar' or 'facial sight,' as it may also be called, is based on the proposition that the human body emits tiny but definite rays of energy of some mysterious variety. These, on coming in contact with a house, wall, car, or any other object are 'bounced back.' A person taught to be attuned to these messages receives them, in some little-understood manner, through the skin or facial nerves. With training, their meaning can be interpreted by the brain—much as sights, sounds, or feelings are interpreted through their own organs. Distance, size, shape and texture can be determined with remarkable accuracy. What happens is that the face, and in some degree the whole body, is converted into a supplementary organ of sense." *

An influential psychologist, who had been concerned over his barren spiritual life, was led into a new, very vital religious experience through the following train of reasoning, which may appeal to other scientific minds:

WHAT SCIENCE KNOWS

Our two billion nerve and brain cells are all miniature electric batteries. Together they produce a magnetic field which we have instruments to measure. Our brains are broadcasting faint radio waves with every thought. Do we also possess receiving sets? Can these be tuned in and can they interpret ideas through radio waves

* From *Everybody's*, London.

from other brains? Yes, this is within the range of possibility. Gray matter under the cortex of the brain is the most sensitive matter known to science, for it is delicate enough to be the home of thoughts. It might just as easily receive messages too delicate for any radio instrument to detect, probably using wave length still unexplored by science. Our knowledge of radio activity is still new and meager. Wave lengths could be used all the way down to electronic waves 1/100,000 as long as light waves.

So there is no reason why the brain's radio waves could not be picked up and correctly interpreted; but *are* they? This is merely a question of cumulative evidence. Telepathy is unquestionably gaining headway, though there are eminent psychologists who regard it as unproven. The experiments of Professor Rhine at Duke University, after the most rigid scrutiny, stand unshaken.

EXPERIMENTERS OUGHT TO PRAY

On the other hand, psychologists who call telepathy unproven have tried experiments with negative results. Perhaps these psychologists omit a factor which Professor Rhine manages to capture—emotional sympathy. His most successful associates are students for the ministry, religiously inclined persons, with complete confidence in one another and unity of spirit. Sympathy and confidence seem to be the radio dials which attune minds to one another. Many laboratory tests which get negative results may be too cold or monotonous for the subconscious minds to make the effort to tune in—just as we turn off radio broadcasts which weary us. Thousands upon thousands of telepathy cases reported by the societies for psychic research are charged with deep feeling between mother and son, man and wife, dear friends.

If sympathy and confidence are the "catalytic agencies" necessary for subconscious minds to venture to tune in, then prayer experiments ought to be far superior to those in a laboratory with cards or other apparatus. People would certainly feel more confidence and eagerness to "turn on their mental receiving sets" if we were praying for their welfare than if we were using them as guinea pigs. Prayer would be the best imaginable key to unlock the defensive suspicion with which people shut themselves from others who are not very near and dear to them. One reason Professor Rhine has succeeded is that he has secured the requisite emotional conditioning in the subconscious minds of his associates.

These considerations led the psychologist to begin praying experimentally. He got the same results as we have here described. But what is even more important, his own relationship with God was transformed. He wrote exultantly: "It is surprising how God can be a reality in one's life and how it is possible to have Him in the background of one's thinking and acting all the time."

The hypotheses about prayer using the same channels as telepathy may turn out to be only half of the truth. Glenn Clark believes that prayer operates at a deeper level than telepathy, at that deepest level where we all flow into God, our great Father. If he is right, then our experiments are at least headed in the right direction.

WE HAVE LANDED ON A NEW CONTINENT

Explorers in the realm of the spirit are like Columbus when he landed on a new continent and did not know what lay beyond. We probably have only just reached the beach-heads of prayer. A vast unknown continent lies beyond us to be explored, conquered and cultivated. Nothing is so thrilling as discovery. Every Christian can and should join in the highest of all adventures in the most wonderful of all worlds, the world of the spirit. Nobody need leave home nor give up his work, for he has his mind with him every minute, and it is in the mind that this exploration is carried on.

Those closing lines of Walt Whitman, in his poem "Passage to India," can be true of us all as we make this fascinating spiritual voyage of discovery:

Sail forth, steer for the deep waters only,
   Reckless, O soul, exploring,
I with thee and thou with me.

For we are bound where mariner has
    not yet dared to go,
And we will risk the ship, ourselves and all.

O my brave soul!
    O farther, farther sail!
O daring joy but safe!
    Are they not all the seas of God,
O farther, farther, farther sail!

✳ IV ✳

Prayer Experiments

THE ELECTRICAL WIZARD Steinmetz said the greatest discoveries of the twentieth century would be in the realm of the spirit. He is right—and ONLY those who pray will make these discoveries. Heaven knows that we need these discoveries now, for we are in the midst of a war to control men's minds. Some of us are tingling with the zest of adventure, for over every hill and around every corner new breath-taking surprises greet our eyes. Adventuring in prayer is exciting fun. God is THERE ahead of us when we walk out in His direction, and God loves surprises and endless variety.

IN THE ALCHEMY STAGE

In the realm of the spirit it is not easy to determine what is truth and what is superstition, because spiritual facts are more difficult to count and hold steady than most physical phenomena. Much of our data concerning spiritual matters is in the same stage as chemistry and medicine were when they were still called "alchemy." Three centuries ago the technique of checking and cross checking physical phenomena had not been developed, and so truth and error were intertangled. We are in that stage yet in many matters of religious experience. Our checking and rechecking of spiritual data is still crude. These data need tests all their own. You cannot put a pin through prayers nor hold them under a microscope, nor dissect them on an operating table. Each of us must go into the laboratory of his own soul, try most of his experiments alone, and exchange notes with other men who are trying similar experiments. Since there is but one witness to the inner experiment, it is liable to faulty observation, faulty memory and unconscious distortion. Words may not mean to the reader what they meant to the writer of the experience.

WHAT RESULTS ARE VISIBLE

Some results can be seen by all men. If prayers are miraculously answered, if divided wills become integrated, if bad men become saints, if the lame walk, or the blind see, we have external evidence which is plain to us all. We need to devise better tests to show what results come from praying for others *at a distance*. The evidence on this question is verifiable. All doubts will be ended not by argument but by experimentation under test conditions. The next few pages suggest some fresh ways of testing intercessory prayer.

MORE TRAINED EXPERIMENTERS NEEDED

A large number of the men who have been trained in scientific method, and who are experimenting with intercessory prayer, must exchange their findings. Only so can we sift the true from the false, and at last describe the laws of prayer for others with greater accuracy. That this field is too sacred to be subjected to experimentation is untrue. The opposite is the truth. Is prayer as vital as the Bible and the church say it is? If so, then everybody needs to be made sure beyond the shadow of doubt. Prayer is too sacred NOT to be given to the entire human race.

NEW NAMES FOR NEW FACTS

Like all discoverers of new things, we shall have to NAME what we discover. In one of the Camps Farthest Out we had great fun suggesting names for the golden bath of love and prayer which surrounded us all week. "You have been swishing prayers at one another and the world all day," the leader said. "You know how it feels; now let us name it!" They made many suggestions like these:

"*Flash* prayers, *scatter* prayers; let prayers *flow* around people or through them; *whisper* prayers, throw a *halo* of prayer or a *prayer cloak* around people; *envelop* them in prayer, *help Christ* inside people, *hold* people and Christ *together*."

Many people think Glenn Clark's *Broadcasting Prayer and Love* is the truest description of the beautiful experience.

THE CAMP BROADCASTS

Under the leadership of Glenn Clark a hundred or more people form circles, or horseshoes, or a V, like the outstretched arms of Christ, and hold hands while they "broadcast." Dramatizing prayer in this fashion induces everybody to participate and stimulates imagination. They imagine their circle transferred to Washington, where it encircles the White House, with the President seated in the center. Then the leader says:

Lord, use this circle as a great funnel through which Thy love can flow to the President. Use us to make him hungry and thirsty for Thy guidance in the vast problems he confronts. Use us to help him hear Thee and do Thy will for the world. We lift him with our hands to Thee and leave him there in Thy presence.

The big circle is then taken in imagination across the Atlantic, to London, and thrown around the Prime Minister of England, where the same prayer is repeated; then to Moscow, and thrown around the Kremlin in Russia; then to China, to India, to Japan, to Germany, and so on to the men and the countries which seem most in need of God's wisdom and help.*

Glenn Clark's camps have seen miraculous happenings during and immediately following their prayer broadcasts, and have been convinced that mass broadcasting changes the very course of history.

OBJECTS FOR WHICH TO PRAY

There are prayer priorities with which we must enlarge our prayers while we continue to pray for our friends, our relatives, and ourselves.

All the following people need to be floodlighted with prayer: The President of the United States and Congress, especially the Senate; the Prime Minister and Parliament of England, Russia's Premier and leaders, China's leaders, delegates at every peace conference, Japanese, Germans, church members and the clergy of Christians and Jews, the missionaries, motion-picture leaders, radio broadcasters, all kinds of slaves and oppressed, Negroes, Americans of Japanese ancestry. We must pray for illiterates, for all teachers, mothers and fathers, for understanding between capital and labor, for human brotherhood, for cooperatives, for the enlarge-

---

* Observe that the above prayer is equally appropriate for every world leader, whether friend or foe. It does not tell God what to do, *it helps men listen while God speaks*. We are like telephone operators at the switchboard; we connect God with people and leave the talking to Him.

ment of people's minds to world vision, for business ethics and for a Christian economic system, for returned soldiers, for children and youth, for wholesome literature, for victims of liquor, drugs and vices of all kinds; for educators and better education. We must pray for hatred to vanish and love to rule the world; we must pray for more *prayer*, for it is the world's mightiest healing force. Doubtless, this long list omits some of your own prayer priorities. Each of us must pray about the themes which he considers most vital, for prayer is valueless unless heart and faith are in it.

Pray with pencil and paper at hand. When God sends a thought, write it down and keep it visible until it can be carried into action. Pray for individuals by name. Vital prayers always suggest things to be done. Indeed, prayer and action must be mates, or both are weak. The mightiest men and women on earth are strong in prayer and strong in deeds. These are the only unbeatable combination.

Glenn Clark, in his *I Will Lift Up Mine Eyes*, tells us how to write out thoughtfully our deepest soul's desires and offer them up to God, and make them a burnt offering in a fireplace. Many who do this say it is uncanny how exactly and completely God answers those prayers. This technique has no magic influence with God, but it does aid our own thinking to be more definite and careful. Many of us are not sure what we think until we have written it down. Most people do not think complete thoughts, but have their heads full of splinters and slivers of thought— broken like a shattered pane of glass. Their prayers, like their thoughts, are usually in splinters. Writing out our thoughts forces us to make them more complete. This does not mean they should be complicated. The clearest thoughts are often written so tersely they snap like a whip. Many perfect prayers can be flashed in ten seconds.

FLASH PRAYERS

To join in the "Praying Ten Million" one need not leave home nor neglect his business. Everybody in every ordinary day has hundreds of chinks of idle wasted time which may be filled with *flash prayers* ten seconds or a minute long. Here are illustrations of such moments:

> Upon awakening in the morning.
> In the bath.
> Dressing.
> Walking down stairs.
> Asking the blessing at table.
> Leaving the house.
> Riding or walking to work.
> Entering the elevator.
> Between interviews.
> Preparing for lunch.
> And a hundred more chinks all day long
>   until crawling into bed and
> Falling asleep. . . .

73

PRAYER

The thousands of people in the United States who travel for religious or charitable purposes, those who sell goods wholesale and retail, insurance men, government officials, soldiers, could make an immense contribution to human progress if they prayed for the strangers around them. *Fanner Bees* in the trains!

It is especially exciting for two persons traveling together, as nuns do, to experiment and share their results.

EXPERIMENTS IN TRAINS AND RESTAURANTS

Some of us who travel much have hundreds of days when we can sit behind people in street cars, trains, stations, restaurants, concerts or lectures, and pray at the backs of their heads with our eyes open to see how many of them show signs of being aware.

Some time ago, I was looking at a man sitting by an open window half a block away. I shot a rapid fire of prayer at him, saying three or four times a second: "Jesus, friend,—Jesus is coming to you." In thirty seconds that man put his head in his hands and bent down over his desk, as though in prayer. Flashing hard and straight prayers in a street car while repeating "Jesus, Jesus, Jesus" usually makes some of the people near you act as though they had been spoken to. If they do not respond the first time, you can

74

return again and again, until they show signs of being "tuned in." They look at you curiously, often smile, and frequently say something. All Christians should acquire this habit. I will try to describe how it feels. It seems to me I am pushing these prayers from my breast and fingers, as well as from my brain—from my whole nervous system. I find myself exhaling a little through my nose with each pressure. After a while, the car or room seems gently "excited," like the magnetic field around a magnet. Everyone behaves like an old friend. People seem to like us to pray for them.

People who are busy reading or talking seem not to respond. That is understandable. All of us have seen how two broadcasting stations, having the same wave length, interfere in our radios. Thoughts can do the same. It is the people whose minds are unoccupied and who are asking, "What next?" who will respond, and often with a quick sharp look of recognition or curiosity.

Far from making one tired, this prayer for others is the finest tonic I know. When you are utterly tired from work or study, walk out into the street and flash prayers at people. Your nerves will tingle with the inflow from heaven. Prayer "is twice blest. It blesses him that gives and him that receives." If you want an experience full of profit and stimulus, take a day off and ride *incognito* in the buses or street cars of your city, flashing strong, fast prayers at people one by one, and noting results. Do this hundreds—if possible, thousands—of times, observing what percentage of them get your broadcast.

SOME STARTLING ANSWERS

I was on a Pennsylvania train praying at the back of a woman's head with a picture of Hoffman's "Boy Christ" in my hand, when she suddenly turned around and said, "What the world needs is more religion."

"Are you a missionary?" I asked her.

"No," she said, "my husband is the conductor."

"You must be a very religious woman," I said.

"No," she replied, "I am a Methodist, but I don't work at it."

"Then why," I asked, "did you say the world needs more religion?"

"I don't know," she replied, "but I just felt like talking about it."

Something of this kind is an everyday occurrence with us who pray for everybody we meet. It *never* happens unless we are praying.

HOW TO KNOW WHEN THEY HEAR YOU

If people reveal no response we cannot conclude that they are unaware. It may be because they repress their impulse to respond. All of us are aware of being gazed at but repress any response unless we are definitely interested, or unless we trust the person gazing at us. We instinctively "play safe." This is why people often do not speak to us when we pray for them (or for that matter, when we say good morning to them). Frequently they betray their awareness by some such response as putting their heads in their hands as in prayer, looking upward and closing their eyes, sighing, looking around, rubbing the back of their heads with their hands, getting up and walking about, shaking their heads sidewise or up and down, a sudden quick jerk as if they had been spoken to.

A railroad station is one of the best places in which to experiment if you have minutes or hours to wait for trains. Fix your eyes on any object you choose, and from that still position try to send a "mental radio field" around in all directions. One seems to "warm up" and gather strength exactly as a radio does when we turn it on. Some of us talk to God about the hopes He has for all the people about us. We send the "still, small" pressure of prayer toward one person at a time, whispering to God or to them, and watching to see who seems to hear and to respond. Only those who try such experiments ever faintly imagine what good prayer in a railroad station can do. At this moment in this station the man opposite me keeps looking at me intently as I write, as though he would ask, "Did you speak to me?" The young woman near me whispered to her soldier friend, and he replied to her aloud, "You're just psychic, that's all." And they both are looking hard at me.

It must be the prayer that does it, for when I do not pray for people they show neither interest nor friendliness. I am personality zero when I do not pray. The moment the prayer pressure starts, the strange, sweet kindliness begins to appear on people's faces and they look at me, ready to talk. If hundreds or thousands of Christian people tried this experiment of "turning on" and "turning off" prayer for those near them, our knowledge of this important matter would vastly increase. And until they do try prayer for others, they miss one of life's richest joys.

All of us have sensed in certain rare persons the strange sense of something we call vaguely "a saintly personality." It develops only in men and women who live by prayer. Science knows little about it, but that proves nothing. Science knows nothing about the nature of such a simple thing as fluorescence, yet many of us have seen it. When we experiment with prayer, we become scientists in the most important and least understood of all fields.

It is time to stop our "conspiracy of silence" about intercessory prayer. "Educated" people have as many taboos as the Hottentots, and this is one of them. Scientific investigation is hampered by the fear of being called a "mystic." For example, not many people would confess the following in public—yet what could be more Christlike?

LOUD SILENCE

The praying—and thinking—of nine people out of ten is too feeble, like a very low-grade broadcasting station. By persistent training we can make our thoughts and prayers louder and reach much farther. Nobody, I think, has yet described any special technique for making our thoughts shout and our prayers broadcast far. That there is a direct relation between intensity and outreach is suggested by the fact that so many people get messages at a great distance when their dear ones are frightened or in an accident.

Some of us, while in a car or bus, fancy our spirts walking over to others and touching them on the shoulder, making some such speech as this: "Christ is in this car. He walks down the aisle to you—and you—and you. He is saying:

> " 'I see in you hidden powers for greater usefulness, personality, happiness, friendship. These beautiful qualities are still in the bud; I will unfold them if you will say *yes*. I will make a wonderful person of you, a blessing to all the world.' "

The subconscious minds of people appear to be eager to hear about Christ's wonderful plans for *their* future. When one silently whispers to them about Christ's hope for them, they sigh and look happy.

THROWING A CLOAK OF PRAYER OVER PEOPLE

When we pray thus toward a man or a group, it feels as though we had thrown a spiritual cloak

79

around our man. When another person is praying for me, I can feel the same spiritual cloak very distinctly enveloping me. I often check this feeling by turning to people and asking, "Did you start to pray for me just then?" and I always have found that I had guessed right. I like the thrill of being prayed for better than anything in the world. If you pray for people, they like it, and so does God like it; for you are helping Him reach them.

On the other hand, all of us dislike being stared at to make us turn around. We may refuse to turn because we are annoyed. It is too much like trying to invade another man's will, and nobody likes to be made a slave.

Moreover, people do not like to be reproved in prayer. If others fail in this experiment, possibly one reason may be that they try to convey ideas disagreeable or irrelevant to the receiver. So if you want your prayers to get by the suspicious guards of other men's unconscious minds, pray for the highest dream you have, and leave out the negatives. Jesus' prayers were all positive.

PRAY WHILE YOU READ

Some of us, while reading newspapers, pause for a second over the names of world leaders in print and whisper, "Lord, may this man be hungry for Thee." Or we simply breathe the word "Jesus" and the man's name together. This will not delay our reading more than a second, and we may be doing great good by holding Jesus and that man together in prayer, even for one second. When this becomes a habit, we shall spread countless thousands of secret blessings over the world, and when millions pray over their newspapers the world may be saved by it.

PRAY WHILE LISTENING TO RADIO MUSIC

When listening to radio music, one may enjoy a very fruitful quarter or half hour, sitting with open or closed eyes and saying silently:

What wilt Thou have me share with Thee now? Think Thy thoughts in my mind. Use me as a channel to make those on the radio hunger and thirst to be closer to Thee, to hear Thee speak, to do Thy will.

PRAY FOR ALL WHOM WE REMEMBER

It is beautiful to acquire the habit of whispering "Jesus" at every person *who comes to memory*. This has a splendid retroactive effect upon ourselves, for it begets love instead of the spirit of criticism. It is a good corrective for that unlovely tendency we have to disapprove of others. The more unattractive people are, the more we need to love them and pray for the ideal they can, by God's help, become. Forget the man as he is, and think vividly of the man he ought to

81

be—and your thought at once begins to force itself into reality.

At last we shall reach a point where only sleep itself interrupts the day full of prayer—sleep, prayer's sunset; awakening, prayer's new sunrise. Then we shall see answers coming in ever-increasing wonder. One's heart aches to find so few who share this ecstasy.

PRAY WHEN AWAKENING AND WHEN FALLING ASLEEP

The moments of falling asleep and awakening are beautiful if they are filled with prayer. We can easily develop the habit, so that closing the eyes at night or opening them at dawn automatically reminds us to pray. "When I awaken I am still with Thee."

When people are unable to sleep at night, they waste millions of hours. We can put these sleepless hours to wonderful usefulness for a better world by praying for every person who comes to mind. For example, "Lord, use my prayer to help Khrushchev to feel hungry and thirsty for Thee; may he hear Thy still, small voice, and obey Thy will."

And so on, and on, perhaps for an hour—turning those fleeting fragments of thought which come when we are half asleep into prayers. The sum total of our prayers, if millions of us learn to do this, will be immense beyond all computation, and their influence incalculable.

PRECEDE, ENFOLD, AND FOLLOW
ALL DEEDS WITH PRAYER

Prayer and action should be wedded. Just as a great surgeon does his best work when praying while he works, so all of us do our best work. Have you not found that when you precede your efforts with prayer, and immerse them in prayer, and follow them with prayer, they always succeed beyond all your expectations? *Prayer is four-fifths of the deed.* When, for any reason, we forget to pray, our efforts are a dud. On the other hand, prayer is weak until we do all we know to help in other ways.

> You can be—yes—you,
> An answer to prayer.
> There is work to be done;
> A field to be won;
> And millions are praying,
> Hands lifted, hearts saying:
> "O Lord, yet how long
> Until right conquer wrong?"
> You can answer that prayer—
> You—answer that prayer.
> —*A. D. Buchet*

E. Harold Bredesen has a clock which his brother rescued from a sinking ship during the war. It strikes every fifteen minutes. Each time it strikes, Bredesen looks at a card on which he has written some cause for which he is praying, and, after a flash prayer, puts the card on the bottom of the pack of prayer cards. His pack

83

of prayer cards keeps growing as he finds new causes for which he desires to pray. This is playing a game with quarter hours!

Another man put more than a thousand photographs of friends on his wall and prayed for them in the darkness throwing a flashlight on each one. There were extraordinary coincidences of friends writing him at the very hour he was praying. Cures of minor illnesses and sharp turns for the better were reported.

Some of us have written to the senators of our own state and to the representative of our own district, telling each of them that we desire to pray for him and asking him if he has a photograph which he will autograph and send us, to help us pray more realistically. Nearly every senator and representative will welcome such a letter and will be helped in his fight with subtle, endless temptations to yield to selfish lobbyists if he realizes that we are praying for him. Enough of us might mold the very course of history by this simple act.

POSITION OF YOUR BODY DOES NOT MATTER

Some people fail to make full use of prayer opportunities because they think they must assume a special position. It is *not* essential in praying to close or raise the eyes, to kneel or stand, to fold the hands or lower the head, nor to make the slightest change of position. However, these customs are all helpful if one is accustomed to them. Some positions are valuable for relaxation of mind and body. But you must never postpone flash prayers until you can find a prayer stool or a chance to close your eyes. You can pray wonderfully while driving an automobile, with your eye on the road every instant.

Rev. Calixto Sanidad, a Filipino saint, wrote: "I used to farm with my hand on the plow, my eyes on the furrow, but my mind on God." That was real. Prayer and work were wedded!

PRAYING WITH THE BODY

Some of us who attend Glenn Clark's camps know how powerful calisthenics can be as an aid to prayer. While pushing our arms full length out, up, front, down, we can repeat rhythmically:

"Lord . . . use—my body—and my—mind— and my—emotions—to help—the President—to hunger—and thirst—to hear—Thee speak—and to—do Thy will."

Glenn Clark writes:

> We discovered that to pray truly, to pray with the greatest abandon and with all of one's power, one should pray with all one's being. It must be a technique that would include one's body as well as one's mind and one's soul.

PRAY WHILE TAKING A WALK

One of the best ways to pray is to take a vigorous walk, talking to God in rhythm with the steps, thus:

Lord, use my prayer—to help these people I am passing—to look up to Thee—to be hungry for Thy voice—to long to do Thy will—to hear Thee speak—to obey Thy voice—to do Thy will.

There is no more exhilarating way of taking exercise than a walking prayer. When your brain is weary, go out into a crowd and waft prayers in all directions; let them trail like a bridal veil, after people as they pass you. You will get the sense that something delicately gauzy, like soft morning light, floats after those for whom you pray. If your experience duplicates mine, you will feel a strange power developing like some long unused muscle. You will be strengthening your soul, just as victims of infantile paralysis strengthen their weak muscles.

If you feel you have cheated yourself in the past by not having a technique in prayer, and if you wish to discipline yourself to this form of prayer, it is simple—so simple that a child can do it. You may say silently with each breath, "Jesus," while you look at the people you meet, trying to help Him reach them. If you think of something else important enough, say it, but if not, the word "Jesus" with every breath is enough. There will never be a more blessed, higher thought to broadcast over the world. Do not strain, for that produces discord.

Then have a notebook to record the instances of observed results.

PRACTICE MAKES PERFECT

Time and again, as you have read these pages, you have probably stopped and prayed. From now on, you must NEVER fail to pray *whenever you think of it,* if only for a second. Habit building is a process of *starting and sticking to it.* If you begin to refuse, refusal becomes habitual, and soon checkmates the habit of prayer. Then you become the victim of an inner conflict between two impulses. The habit of praying is simple and unstrained, unless you allow it to be complicated by *exceptions* and *refusals.* If you keep sending flash prayers every time you think about it, without ever an exception, after a while you will find it is second nature. Any normal person can develop a habit of making every glance at another a gentle pressure of prayer, until, at last, the whole day is as full of little prayers as the sky is full of stars. There develops a sweet flowing into us from God, and an endless flowing out toward humanity. The quiet rhythm of heaven can be ours in the midst of a crowded, troubled, and desperate world. And the terrible world itself gradually changes around us when we live in His peace.

Our prayer may seem to be weak at first, but as we practice with thousands upon thousands of these flash prayers, we feel them grow in power, we feel them COME BACK TO US like radar. When that happens our hearts skip a beat with the thrill of it, for we know that we are learning to be channels for God, and, what is more, that we are children of God, working with Him for His Kingdom plan.

The blinding realization that by letting Him use us we can help save the world forces upon us an all-demanding challenge. It presses upon our time, every moment of it, as the air presses every moment against the wings of a plane, holding it to its high course.

TEACH YOUTH TO PRAY FREQUENTLY

A progressive American educator said: "Instead of teaching young people to listen to long prayers and longer sermons on Sunday morning, teach them to make brief sentence prayers many times a day; teach them that prayer is the best way to meet every need and every task."

Youth has a thousand times more mental and physical energy than Protestant churches have helped them use creatively. If high-school boys and girls are taught that by praying for leaders they actually mold world history, they pray with all the reckless abandon of youth. This sense that they can DO SOMETHING VITAL rescues them from cynicism, enlarges their world view, creates interest in really important affairs, keeps them close to God, makes them ambitious to serve, gives them a sense of mission, and saves them from throwing their lives away in cheap sin. American youth need a powerful Cause and a program they can undertake at once. Prayer for everybody is one such program, and saving our age is the Cause!

And we adults need that Cause just as much as youth, especially people over sixty. On every hand, one sees elderly people resigning from their work in order to "enjoy life during my last years." Most of them are lost and unhappy and in a few months they are likely to pine away and die. Joining the prayer army is their best hope, and if they know how prayer changes the world they will tingle with the sense of helping God.

V

Christ—the Answer

NEW KNOWLEDGE CORROBORATES JESUS

MODERN PSYCHOLOGY bears out every word Jesus said about thoughts, with sledge-hammer emphasis. Every man's thinking takes on world-wide importance. EVERY evil thought not only contaminates the man himself, but makes the world worse, pushes it toward hell. Every good thought not only blesses the man himself but also pushes the entire world up toward heaven.

So Jesus plunges deep into the mind, the source of all action. He said, in effect, "You have heard that it was said by them of old time, Thou shalt not commit adultery; But I say unto you *Do not lust*. Ye have heard Do not kill, but I say *Do not hate*." Because every theft, every lie, every vulgar word, and every murder comes from evil ideas.

Again, "You wash the exterior of the cup and saucer, but inside you are full of licentiousness and rapine. You are like white tombs, outside lovely, but *inside* full of bones of death and filth. Outside you appear just, but *inside* you are full of hypocrisy and wickedness." This is what Jesus was saying to the Pharisees. His words are just as true for our day. "This people," He said, "honor me with their lips, but their *minds* are far from me and in vain they worship me."

The Jews of His day supposed that eating pork poisoned the soul and the body, but Jesus told them: "Nothing that enters the mouth contaminates a man, but what comes out contaminates the man; because from the mind proceed bad thoughts, murders, adulteries, fornications, thefts, false testimonies, blasphemies. These are the things which defile a man."

Several times Jesus repeated these words: "A good man out of the good *treasure* of his heart bringeth forth good things; and an evil man out of the evil treasure bringeth forth evil things."

A CLEAN MIND IS GOOD BUT NOT GOOD ENOUGH

It isn't enough to cleanse the mind of evil thoughts, though that is essential. An empty mind will not stay empty, or clean! Jesus' strange parable about a devil which left a man's mind and came back with seven more devils was exactly to the point. The demons found the man's mind cleansed and a vacuum, so they rushed in. The only way to keep out demonic ideas is to have the mind full of "a good treasure" of thoughts, vital, burning thoughts, big enough to fill the mind and heart.

Moreover, a clean empty mind is purely negative and useless to others. It does nothing to fight or cancel out the active burning hate-thoughts which curse our world.

That is why Paul was speaking a truth he got straight from Jesus when he said:

> Whatsoever things are true, whatsoever things are honest, whatsoever things are just, whatsoever things are pure, whatsoever things are lovely, whatsoever things are of good report; if there be any virtue, and if there be any praise, think on these things.

If people have any virtue, *praise* it, says Paul rightly, and forget their weaknesses. For whatever we think about we fan into a flame, whether we think *for* it or *against* it.

NO NEW BRILLIANT THOUGHTS ARE NEEDED

It is not necessary for our thoughts to be NEW thoughts. Indeed, new ideas are not what we need at this moment, not even new good ones! Decades would pass before our new ideas would be accepted by the multitudes and before we could find out whether they were really workable. We cannot wait for decades. Now is when our world needs help—NOW!

Besides, most new ideas prove to be wrong. They are like the "sports" in the plant world which appear in such profusion when electricity is applied to plants—only one new mutation in a million is a real improvement. The rest are inferior or monstrosities. Machiavelli and Nietzsche had an idea. When Hitler tried it on the world he dragged it into horror. We must suspect all new thoughts until they have been tested in the light of the life and teachings of Jesus. He and His way must become master of the Kingdom, and every thought must come into harmony with Christ.

CHRIST'S TEACHING IS THE WORLD'S HOPE

Fortunately, the knowledge that can save the world is already ours. It is the way of Jesus Christ, what He is, what He teaches, and how He transforms men. When we join our thoughts to Him we are in an immense river, pouring through every race and every nation. Jesus has already proven to be the world's greatest blessing. He has not yet been able to save it from its present state, because not enough of us are thinking and acting upon His ideals. You and I and all true Christians confess that we have done far below our best. When we get behind the stupendous ongoing Christian current, we aid the only program which has any hope of saving our generation.

Christ is not only the most *powerful* person the world has known; He is the noblest. All the highest ideals since His day, as H. G. Wells declared, have sprung from His teachings. What is more, Jesus Himself lived His ideals even better than He could find words to express them. Nine-tenths of the human race would follow Christ if they knew what He is, when they would not follow an abstract truth.

BECOMING CHRIST-SATURATED

But how shall we help all men to know Him? That was Paul's question, and it still is ours. The greatest way to help Christ conquer the world is to saturate our own minds with Him. We do this by thinking about Christ and His Kingdom *as much as we can*. If we think about Him we shall inevitably witness for Him and work for Him. Other people will catch Him from us by our deeds and words. "Out of the fullness of the heart the mouth speaketh." But, equally important, they will catch our thoughts telepathically, just as advertisers send their messages out over the radio, in the knowledge that tens of thousands of people will tune in sooner or later. If we keep Him in our thoughts persistently all day, every day, we shall radio thoughts of Christ to the minds of countless millions all over the world.

HIS LIFE IN THE GOSPELS

How can we saturate our minds with Christ? There is but one way to get a true picture of Him. This is to read His life in the four Gospels so often that we know it by heart. We who wish to be Christlike ought never to allow a day to pass without reading at least a chapter of the Gospels. We get the best results if we take a definite hour (and a fresh hour) every day. The last hour before going to bed is poor, especially after a hard day's work, for we are likely to fall asleep half way through a chapter. Many of the spiritual giants read their Bibles at four or five every morning, before others can disturb them.

To prevent this reading from becoming tedious, many of us, after finishing the Gospels in the familiar text, use fresh translations—the Revised Standard Version, Goodspeed, Moffatt, Weymouth. AFTER we have these Gospels practically memorized in English, a good way to learn a new language, like Spanish, French, or Chinese, is to read the Gospels in that language. Lord Macaulay read the Hindu New Testament while on the way to India, and surprised the Indians by speaking and reading their language upon his arrival.

We need determined wills to protect this hour with Christ from competing interests. Busy people are under constant temptation to allow Bible reading to be crowded out every other day, until omission becomes a habit. Then they find the edge of their interest dulling and their attention wavering. The *only* protection we have is to consider this hour of devotions a sacred engagement with God, and to decline all interrupting invitations. Even better is family Bible reading and prayer as a solemn daily engagement.

HAVING OUR SHRINES AT HOME

Many of us, like the Roman Catholics, can pray better if we look at a shrine. Most Protestant churches are now using altars.

If we ought to "pray without ceasing," then we need shrines to remind us of Christ wherever we spend our time. We can construct little shrines for ourselves instantly at home or in a hotel room by placing a cross or the open Bible in front of our favorite picture of Christ. Some of us travelers have a picture folder containing pictures of Christ which we unfold and stretch across our dressers whenever we reach a new city. One Christian leader has a large globe, with an electric light inside, to represent "The Light of the World."

Many Christians have pictures of a friendly Christ in every room in the house, including the bathroom, to serve as reminders for their treacherous memories. The Catholics, with crosses around their necks to remind them of Christ, are using better psychology than those of us who use no helps and who never pray. Better to walk with crutches than not at all.

FILLING THE CHINKS OF TIME

While a daily devotional hour is vital for saturating our minds with Christ, *it is not enough.* All during the day, *in the chinks of time* between the things we find ourselves obliged to do, there are moments when our minds ask: "What next?" In these chinks of time, ask Him:

"Lord, think Thy thoughts in my mind. What is on Thy mind for me to do now?"

When we ask Christ, "What next?" we *tune in* and give Him a chance to pour His ideas through our enkindled imagination. If we persist, it becomes a habit. It takes some effort, but it is worth a million times what it costs. It is possible for *everybody, everywhere*. Even if we are surrounded by throngs of people we can continue to talk silently with our invisible Friend. We need not close our eyes nor change our position nor move our lips.

HOW WE THINK CHRIST'S THOUGHTS

Thinking about Christ constantly is easy to understand. It is not easy to do. Yet there is a way to do it without stopping our other occupations. It is to acquire a new way of thinking. Thinking is a process of talking to your "inner self." Instead of talking to yourself, talk to the Invisible Christ. If you do that all day every day, then your thoughts are spreading Christ all over the planet wherever other minds are tuned in to yours. Hundreds of thousands, or perhaps millions, of minds will be better. You become what George Eliot described in her "Choir Invisible":

The sweet presence of a good diffused,
And in diffusion even more intense!

So shall I join the choir invisible
Whose music is the gladness of the world.

HOW TO HOLD A CONVERSATION WITH CHRIST

Prayer at its highest is a two-way conversation. You may say silently or aloud, "Lord, what art Thou saying to me?" Then let your imagination perfectly loose while you reply to yourself what you SUPPOSE He would answer. You may imagine Him saying:

"This is for you and for everybody. I have been waiting for this moment all your life, waiting until you opened the channel so that I could speak. I have wonderful plans for you which cannot be realized until you listen as you are listening now. The trouble with all the world is that people do not stop to listen while I speak. . . ."

Thought transformed into conversation with Christ becomes larger, more unselfish, more worth-while, purer, more noble. Try it!

WHEN TIRED

When the mind is too weary to do hard thinking or praying, the loveliest word we can allow to float through our thoughts is "Jesus, Jesus, Jesus. Sweetest name on mortal tongue, sweetest name by angels sung, Jesus, precious Jesus." Many a dear mother of mediocre ability, walking through life, whispering, "Jesus" every moment will do more to sweeten and save humanity than all the cunning schemes of diplomats or the fine-spun guesses of philosophers who leave Jesus out. Just to think of others and whisper, "Jesus," is the noblest contribution most of us can ever make to other lives as well as our own. The spiritual life is a true democracy, for it is as freely given to the humble and unlearned as to the scholar!

MAKING IT A HABIT

If we have had a lifetime habit of thinking *with Christ left out* we shall find the old habit stubborn. It is as difficult to learn the new way to think as it is to learn to typewrite or to play a piano or to learn a new language. We do it haltingly and rather feebly the very first time, like taking the first lessons in any high art. We must not underestimate the time required to become proficient, or we may say impatiently, "It can't be done," which is sheer nonsense. It can't be done *well* in a day. It can't be learned *perfectly* in a year. But it can become nearly perfect in ten years. Meanwhile, the progress from day to day is so thrilling, and the satisfactions so wonderful, that every day is a joy. Perhaps we do other people more good while we are still learners than after we have become perfect, for we understand their difficulties and they understand ours. "The best teacher is he who is also a learner."

Even after a lifetime of prayer, the saints realize that they do not fully attain the perfect surrender of Christ to the thought of God. There will always be heights for us to attain—and that adds to the zest of living.

JESUS KEPT HIS MIND IN PERFECT SURRENDER

Forty-seven times in the Gospel of John, Jesus said He was under God's orders, and that He never *did* anything, never *said* anything, until His Father gave the command. He was listening every moment of the day to His invisible companion and saying, "Yes." This perfect obedience was what made Him one with His Father and what gave the Father perfect confidence in the Son. It is the reason the Father loves His Son so fondly. This is exactly what the Gospel of John declares that Jesus said over and over and over. Here are typical passages:

John 5:19: "The Son can do nothing of himself [nothing!] but what he seeth the Father do; for what things soever he doeth, these also doeth the Son likewise."

5:30: "I can of mine own self do nothing: . . . I seek not mine own will, but the will of the Father which hath sent me."

7:16: "My doctrine is not mine, but his that sent me. (28) . . . and I am not come of myself. . . . (29) . . . for I am from him, and he hath sent me. . . . (33) . . . and then I go unto him that sent me."

8:16: ". . . for I am not alone, but I and the Father that sent me. (26) . . . and I speak to the world those things which I have heard of him. (28) . . . I do nothing of myself. . . . (29) And he . . . is with me: the Father hath not left me alone; for I do always those things that please him."

10:17: "Therefore doth my Father love me, because I lay down my life. . . . (18) No man taketh it from me, but I lay it down of myself. . . . This commandment have I received of my Father."

10:38: ". . . the Father is in me, and I in him. (30) I and my Father are one."

At the heart of the universe is this wonderful, never-ending harmony, this incredible love between Father and Son. 17:10: ". . . I have kept my Father's commandments and abide in his love. 16:15: All things that the Father hath are mine. . . ." Jesus had earned the confidence and love of His Father, and so the world could be entrusted to Him as His responsibility.

WE ARE INVITED TO JOIN THEM

Into that wonderful loving family we are invited, not as servants but as brothers of Christ, as sons of God. This is what Jesus says over and over in many ways. It is what He came for.

John 13:15: ". . . I have given you an example, that ye should do as I have done to you."

14:23: "If a man love me, he will keep my

words: and my Father will love him, and we will come unto him, and make our abode with him."

15:14: "Ye are my friends, if ye do whatsoever I command you. (10) If ye keep my commandments, ye shall abide in my love; even as I have kept my Father's commandments, and abide in his love. (16) . . . I have chosen you . . . that ye should go and bring forth fruit, and that . . . whatsoever ye shall ask of the Father in my name, he may give it you."

SONS OF GOD

This incredible invitation to be more than an angel, to be a *son* along with Christ the Son, a member of the Holy Family, is all summed up in a few verses (Jesus is praying to His Father)— John 17:21: "That they all may be one; as thou, Father, art in me, and I in thee, that they also may be one in us: . . . (23) I in them and thou in me, that they may be made perfect in one. . . . thou . . . hast loved them, as thou hast loved me. (24) Father, I will that they also, whom thou hast given me, be with me where I am. . . . (26) . . . that the love wherewith thou hast loved me may be in them, and I in them."

We are invited to the center of the wonderful love at the heart of the universe, not merely as an onlooker but as a "son." Words could not be plainer. This is what Jesus came down from heaven for: "to them gave he power to become the sons of God. . . ." That is the most audacious

103

conception that ever entered the human mind.
"I," said Christ, in effect, "am God's son, but *so
are you!*"

After the resurrection He said (John 20:17):
". . . I ascend unto my Father, and your Father;
and to my God, and your God." He invites us to
His side. It is a family, a father and his children
—we are God's family.

That is all one can make of these startling
words which Jesus quoted when they accused
Him of blasphemy for calling Himself the "Son
of God." John 10:34-36: "Is it not written in
your law, I said, Ye are gods? If he called them
gods, unto whom the word of God came. . . .
Say ye of him, whom the Father hath sanctified,
and sent into the world, Thou blasphemest; because I said I am the Son of God?" This could
mean but one thing: so are you a son of God if
you obey the Father perfectly, as Jesus did!

HOW WE EARN SONSHIP

We *earn* this inner place with Father and Son
at the center of the universe, the same way Jesus
earned it. We earn it by perfect obedience, the
kind Jesus gave His Father every minute and
every second. But for us this is the obstacle in
Jesus' invitation—and it is a very formidable
hurdle. For when one undertakes to listen and
obey as incessantly as Jesus listened and obeyed,
one finds it almost impossible. We can go through
the better part of some days perfectly surren-

dered, but eventually we forget or politely bow Christ and the Father out, while we indulge in some useless nonsense, perhaps something we know He would not tell us to do. We use our time one way, while, if we were listening to Him, He would tell us to use it differently. This is unlike Jesus who said: "I do *nothing* of myself." It is the difference between an utterly dependable character and a wobbly character.

Nearly all of our lapses are pure forgetfulness. Often our subconscious minds play us a trick and make us forget intentionally. This inconstancy of ours is the chief reason why the promises of Jesus are untrue to our experience, why we ask for so much that does not happen. Of course, it doesn't happen when we are apart from Christ. ". . . apart from me," He said, "ye can do nothing . . ." (PHILLIPS). His incredibly sweeping promises depend upon our staying with Him as a branch stays with the vine. "As the branch cannot bear fruit of itself, except it abide in the vine; no more can ye, except ye abide in me. . . . If ye abide in me, and my words abide in you, ye shall ask what ye will, and it shall be done unto you" (John 15:4, 7). You who read this know that our failure is at this point—our minds are busy with many other things, and we pull loose from the vine many times, probably most of the time every day. What branch grafted on a tree could flourish if we pulled it loose every day to see whether it was growing? It would soon be dead!

PRAYER

Several persons who have read my booklet, *The Game with Minutes,* advocating an attempt to think of God at least one second in each minute, have written that they found it so beyond them that they gave up trying and decided that they were not "built to be saints." A few, given to taking life very seriously, were inclined to be self-condemnatory. Several persons say that it saved them from insanity. Others say it saved them from being introverts. The "game with minutes" is well named a *GAME,* a game which practically nobody wins *all* the time.

Yet *everybody* really wins it who tries, for he *does better* than he would have done without a trial. James Russell Lowell said: "Not failure but low aim is crime." When we fail to make a high score, let us laugh and start all over afresh—for, you see, WE HAVE ETERNITY, so long as we are *headed in the right direction,* and a few hours lost does *not* mean that *we* are lost. It means that we are building spiritual muscle, that we are trying something worthy of our *best* possibilities. We grow to the stature of our goals. Without a goal to keep us trying our souls atrophy like unused muscles.

BEGIN OVER INSTANTLY!

God forgives us instantly and eagerly. Let's forgive ourselves! To "repent" does not mean to "repine," but to "right about face and start moving in the right direction." Christ's joy is in helping men make new beginnings. He finds no pleasure in condemning. He delights only in helping us rise higher. No matter what the last hour may have been, it is past, and we live in this moment, to make it as fine as we can in thought and deed. Never let the sins or errors of the last hour poison this! "Snap out of it" instantly, and, lo, a new fresh page is turned. He who adopts the philosophy of instantaneous new beginnings has the secret of peace.

The most subtle of all forms of selfishness is over-anxiety for *ourselves* to be *more perfect* than other people; not desiring that our neighbor shall be as perfect as we are. The quest for self-perfection is often sanctified introversion. The ideal is to forget self as Mary did, sitting at the feet of Jesus, and to gaze enraptured "full in His glorious face," *listening* for His whisper and *doing all He asks*. This is what Jesus does with His Father every moment.

PLAYING LIFE'S GAME WITH A SMILE

American leaders are nearly always photographed with a smile on their faces. That is the way to greet every day, with a smiling face and a singing heart. Life is our great game, and it's fun to play it the best we can. Temporary defeats never matter unless we fret about them, unless they keep us down!

Robert Browning struck the brave, healthy note:

One who never turned his back but marched breast
    forward,
  Never doubted clouds would break,
Never dreamed, though right were worsted, wrong
    would triumph,
Held we fall to rise, are baffled to fight better,
  Sleep to wake. . . .
For we have eternity!

If we can't play ANY game for the sheer fun of it, we ought not to play it at all. But we must all play this game with life, so let's do it with a light in our eyes and a song on our lips. We have every good reason to be radiant. We are undefeatable—unless we defeat ourselves. And even then we can begin all over in an instant—this instant!

Thank God, one needs no unusual ability to be full of Christ, one need not profess unusual goodness, nor worthiness, nor an unusual past, nor blue blood, nor social connections, nor money. The Gospel is for everybody, and "no questions asked."

Listen and say, "Yes." Enter God's open doors unafraid. He is there waiting. "Down God's street there are always green lights." What an undefeatable Gospel!

A friend remonstrated, "You make it altogether too easy. This is the hardest achievement on earth and your light-hearted promises will deceive people."

Very well, then, let us say plainly it *does cost*. You have got to *stop loving things and yourself*. There is no substitute for that. Worshiping mammon and self is of all ways of living the most wretched. Let go courageously of *self* and *things*, and, lo! it is as easy to begin living with Him as breathing. The final goal is far, far away, but every step with Him toward that goal is heavenly!

VI

Our Appalling Power

EVERY THOUGHT IS A DEED

WHEN ROOSEVELT, CHURCHILL, and Stalin were holding their fateful conferences during the Second World War they must have had an overwhelming sense of their responsibility to bless or curse the entire world. If mental radio operates between people, it means that *everybody* has an overwhelming responsibility for good and evil. It means that every thought we think is helping or harming other people. If you shout, your voice carries barely fifty yards. But when you think, your thoughts go around the world, as far and as fast as the radio. The thoughts of a single day pour blessings or cursings into the great river of world opinion. Every man, in the course of a lifetime, pours so many million thoughts for good or ill into the ever-moving stream of human history that he leaves his impress upon the world as long as time lasts. This is literally and terribly true if thoughts do leap from one mind to another.

If you and I are convinced that we are all so connected, we must never harbor a thought that would poison others; we must try to think

PRAYER

Thoughts sublime that pierce the sky like stars
And by their mild persistence urge men on
To vaster issues.

The ordinary thoughts of good men are *good little thoughts*. The extemporaneous prayers one hears in public are like most thinking, full of "miserable aims that end in self."

The most acute need of our age is for global-minded people who "think the world thought, do the world deed, and pray the world prayer."

DO WE INFLUENCE NATURE WHEN WE PRAY?

Does God change the course of nature when we pray? This is not a question to be decided by logic. It is a question of fact. It is ridiculous to ask whether God COULD change the usual course of nature, although science used to say the laws of nature could not be broken. Has He done so or hasn't He? *If He does, He does.* And it seems He does now as surely and perhaps as often as He did in Christ's day. Who of us have prayed without receiving some startling answer? You could not persuade most soldiers otherwise. Either our wars have produced more liars than you could count, or miracles *have* happened. Fish have jumped into boats, birds have landed on men's heads, and strange winds have blown boats to shore. . . .

Let one story illustrate: it was written by

Sergeant Johnny Bartek, a companion of Captain Eddie Rickenbacker:

> As soon as we were in the rafts at the mercy of God, we realized that we were not in any condition to expect help from Him. We spent many hours of each day confessing our sins to one another and to God. . . .
>
> Then we prayed,—and God answered. It was real. We needed water. We prayed for water and we got water—all we needed. Then we asked for fish, and we got fish. And we got meat when we prayed. Sea gulls don't go around sitting on people's heads waiting to be caught! On that eleventh day when those planes flew by, we all cried like babies. It was then I prayed again to God and said: "If you'll send that one plane back for us I promise I'll believe in you and tell everyone else." That plane came back and the others flew on. It just happened? It did not! God sent that plane back!

Our hard-headed psychologist would find it hard to explain all that by "mental radio." Telepathy might have called the pilot in the airplane and even the sea gulls, and the fish—but hardly the rain!

Yet—Professor Rhine of Duke University is finding that when he and his associates concentrate while dice are being thrown, the dice tend to obey their wills.* If that be true then there is

* *American Magazine*, September, 1944.

much we do not know. We are on the beach-
heads of a vast new continent and cannot safely
dream what may lie ahead!

CO-CREATORS WITH GOD

Since *every thought* is creative, we are creators
of the world—we, along with God. He began
the world well without us, but we help Him now
—and that is the trouble! We humans helped
create the world of 1944 by what we thought
and planned since World War I. Our end of
creation has been pretty bad—that is the reason
we have been through this war. The warped little
thoughts of selfish, contemptible men from 1918
to 1940 made World War II—and not all of them
were on the Axis side. Nothing brought us to
the brink of hell but warped, prejudiced, greedy
little thoughts.

And now, in 1960, our thoughts, large and
small, are at work making the world of 1980.
There are two reasons for this:

1. Every thought *tends to become true* in proportion as it is intense and as it is long dwelt upon.
Thoughts result in deeds and deeds make history.

2. Our thoughts *leap across space* and appear
again in other minds, in proportion as they are
intense and long dwelt upon. Thoughts are con-
tagious. "What you whisper in secret," said Jesus,
"shall be shouted from the housetops." Yes, even
your thoughts shout, though others may not
know it is you who are shouting!

"I SAID YE ARE GODS"

The Greeks believed that the gods were on Olympus, but if Jesus is correct, then God has set millions of little gods free on this earth to help create whatever we think about. We are "sons of God" with a vengeance. Our thoughts are the threads weaving the garment which the world tomorrow will wear. You and I created a piece of tomorrow in our thoughts today. We cannot help ourselves. We are gods without knowing it —even if we refuse to believe it. There is no escape from this responsibility; we have got to measure up.

RIGHT AND WRONG ARE NEARLY BALANCED

You and I need to ask: "When my thoughts come true, and when they leap around the world to start the same thoughts moving in other minds, are my thoughts making the kind of world we really want?" I am only one of two billion of the world's population to be sure, but my thoughts are as creative as any of the others, and *so are yours*. The human race—if we may judge by what people read and say and do—are a mixture of good and evil thoughts, large and little thoughts. If they could be checked over against each other they might pretty much cancel out. One may "guestimate" that the sum total of right and wrong thinking is nearly in balance, like a balloon suspended in air, hesitating whether to rise or fall. Our world seems to rise for a period, then to fall, then to rise again. If a few millions of us determine to keep our thoughts right all the time, we can, I believe, tip the balances the other way, and, by God's help, start our bad old globe rising instead of falling. If this earth is indeed in a state of *near balance*, then your thinking and mine may be decisive, may save the world from a worse hell. We don't know how much good we may be able to do by keeping our thoughts high and large and creative—we do know that *all of us are important*. God only knows how important we are.

WE HAVE DELAYED GOD

That excellent anonymous book, *God Calling*, puts in the mouth of Christ these words:

> I do not delay my second coming, my followers delay it. . . . The world would be brought to me soon if only all who acknowledge me as Lord and Christ gave themselves unreservedly to be used by me. . . . I could use each human body as a channel for divine love and power.

The same picture fills the Bible, the picture of God, heartbroken and delayed by man's disobedience. This is the eternal meaning of Adam thrown out of Eden. This is what the flood at the time of Noah means, when "God repented

him that he had made man." The story of the
forty years in the wilderness says plainly God
was delayed. The captivity in Babylon means a
delayed and disappointed God. The story is written on nearly every page of the prophets. Christ
spoke for the God of the whole Bible when He
wept over Jerusalem: ". . . how often would I
have gathered thy children together, even as a
hen gathereth her chickens under her wings, and
ye would not! Behold, your house is left unto
you desolate" (Matthew 23:37, 38).

Is our world headed for destruction, or can it
be saved? *Perhaps God has not yet made up His
mind;* perhaps He lets our actions decide, perhaps
His plan is to let us make up our minds. This is
what He does with individuals—"Whosover will
may come." It may be that this is His way with
nations and eras—to let us pronounce our own
judgment. It looks as though He will allow this
generation to destroy itself if we cannot join
hands in brotherly co-operation. It would be easy
to quote fifty pages from the prophets, who, like
Ezekiel 18, say exactly that. They say it, not only
about individuals, but also about their nation
Israel. The whole Bible plays around the word
"if," and the doubtful element is what men will
at last do. If, if, if!!! Unless, unless, unless!!!
God's will is clear—man's will hangs in the balance, and man's decision in this generation decides
this generation's fate. That is precisely the message of the Bible, and it is most certainly the

message of science. God's laws are immutable. Obey and live, or disobey and be ground to powder.

This judgment does not depend upon outward deeds alone. It plunges into the depths of the mind: "For the word of God is quick, and powerful, and sharper than any twoedged sword, piercing even to the dividing asunder of soul and spirit, and of the joints and marrow, and is a discerner of the thoughts and intents of the heart. . . . all things are naked and opened unto the eyes of him with whom we have to do" (Hebrews 4:12, 13).

Somebody cringes at this terrible responsibility. "You are saying that I help decide my world's fate. But I'm powerless to do anything about it." Powerless? On the contrary, you are *enormously powerful*. Your thinking this very day has helped make the world what it is. When you think in perfect harmony with God, the titanic forces of the universe bend like gravity to pull things and people in your direction, because you are going in God's direction. One man with God shall be stronger than ten thousand!

THE GREATEST TRUTH IN THE WORLD

You and I will be responsible for 1980, and even though we deny our blame, that does not change the facts. There is but one escape, not to dodge, but to rise to the challenge. If this is true at all, it becomes the most vital truth in the universe for us and for everybody. What could be more awe-inspiring, more heart-gripping, more overmastering, more terrifying? The universe pays the price if you and I fail to measure up to our highest!

The sheer responsibility of this realization might drive one mad if it were not for the one redeeming fact that by the help of Christ WE CAN think His thoughts. When we share our thoughts with Him, the enormous responsibility for the future of the world rolls over on His shoulders. He carries what is too big for us, and He supplies the power. St. Paul's marvelous words, as translated by Goodspeed, are true: "God working through us is able to do unutterably more."

Whenever man opens the windows of his mind toward God, then God tells him what to do, and helps him to do it. That man thinks and does "unutterably more."

WE CAN! ENOUGH OF US CAN!

We CAN! We don't need to wait! It's in our power NOW! We can have a world of peace, justice, happiness, the Kingdom of God as soon as we want it. Every new scientific discovery can bend to aid humanity if people will love Christ and one another. But we must pay a price, just as soldiers must give up all they cherish. We must give up most of our ordinary little thinking for the world's sake.

Non-Christians constitute no more than half of

God's problem. Christians who sit on the side lines and who do not help, are the other half of His problem. It isn't that they can't, it isn't that they won't, it is just that they *don't*, because they *don't know how*. Many more of us would "get into the game" if we saw how *important, how terrifyingly important*, each of us is for the saving of our generation; if we saw how easy it would be for us to help tip the scales toward the Kingdom of God; if we saw that *all the time, no matter where we are*, our right thinking builds a bridge between God and other men—the bridge that God *needs* if His Will is to be done on earth and if this generation is to be saved from destroying itself.

ENOUGH OF US COULD TRANSFORM THE WORLD RIGHT NOW

We have enough Christian people to transform the world right now, if only their thoug's were always on Christ's side. But they supp se their thoughts are their own, and so a large part of their thinking cancels out the rest of their thinking. Many people enjoy dreaming about the wicked deeds they are condemning in other people; that is why scandal is so popular! If our postulate is correct, we help evil even when we roll it around under our tongues in delicious hypocritical disapproval of others. We need to mobilize the minds of the men of good will so that they will form a mighty *mass attack of good*

120

thoughts. Then we all together will tip the scales the other way, will lift the world upward to a new high, in spite of the selfish little thoughts of mean people.

Here is a principle most people need:

Fix your thoughts upon what ought to come to pass, and not upon the things you dislike. Let the things we oppose die of neglect. For we help everything we think about—even when we are thinking against it!

THE REACTION OF GOOD THOUGHTS UPON OURSELVES

Some readers of this book may be murmuring: "There is scarcely a word about what prayer and right thinking will do for ME! It is all about what I can do for *others*." That omission was deliberate. There are enough books already on helping *yourself* through prayer—on how to get what you want, how to acquire riches, how to find health, how to be famous, how to go to heaven. But in this era, when our bleeding world faces the worst crisis in history, when it calls like a drowning man, it is contemptibly selfish to ask what advantage will come to *us* if we go to her rescue.

Nevertheless, this much may be said. The habit of praying for others makes you noble.

Your thoughts grow wider and higher,

Your selfishness melts away.

You become Christlike.

You bless mankind.

You are loved by all who know you.

People think you are beautiful, for

You become radiant with the smile of Christ.

Your joy comes from what you give, not from
what you accumulate.

"He that loseth his life shall find it."

Take no thought for your own life, what you shall eat and wear. "Seek ye first the kingdom of God and his righteousness, and all these things shall be added unto you."

Let us dismiss these personal considerations with a paragraph and train our sights once more upon helping others. We are needed as channels between God's power and the world's need. The more we think about self, the more we block the channel between God and His world. The more we eliminate self, the wider becomes our channel of blessing to others. Men's refusal to help others unless they get praise or profit is God's "bottle-neck" as He strives to bring in the Kingdom. God's greatest need is more than unselfishness, it is selflessness, wide-open channels for His love.

There is a well-known fable of heaven and hell. In hell they sit on both sides of a table, but their arms are straight and stiff, so that they cannot get the food to their mouths. In heaven they sit around the same kind of table with the same straight arms, but with one difference—they feed one another across the table. That fable is not true of heaven and hell, but it is true of our earth now. All hunger is because we are too selfish to feed one another. Our thoughts and even our prayers have been *too self-centered.*

God has permitted science to unlock the ultimate forces locked in the atom, thirty million times as powerful as dynamite. Now scientists are frightened lest men may use this awful power to destroy the world. Prayer will enable God to unlock in the spiritual realm the only power that can save the human race from destroying itself. This is the one and only great contribution most of us can make, and it is enough.

THIS IS THE UNTRIED WAY

Your contribution can be titanic beyond all imagination. It depends upon one thing only— how much *time* and *heart* and *mind* and *soul* and *strength* and *prayer* you give to *God's world task.*

If true at all, the truth in this book is the most important of all truths. God's thoughts, plus ours, create the future! Even fools dare not turn their backs on this terrific challenge. All of us must stop being vindictive, stop being prejudiced, stop being little; for our folly, our spite, our prejudice, our narrowness are poisoning the universe. We must think thoughts worthy of the sons of God, worthy of creators of the world of 1980, and beyond.

Well, then, let us pray:

God, use my prayer to help the delegates and officials of the United Nations to feel a sense of awful need for Thy wisdom. May they pray, listen to Thee intently, hear Thee correctly, and obey Thee perfectly. Use my prayer to give Christians everywhere a sense of awful responsibility to pray, to listen to Thee and hear Thee right, and obey Thee fully. Use me as an open channel for an outpouring of the Holy Spirit upon mankind.

We are confident that you have found in this famous book inspiration and challenge; answers to some of your questions concerning prayer. Share your experience with a friend—give this enduring classic . . . now in a deluxe, gift edition.

Mail this coupon today to your bookseller

GENTLEMEN:

PLEASE SEND ME

____ COPIES PRAYER, *The Mightiest Force in the World*

BY *Frank C. Laubach* @ $2.50 EACH (*gift edition*)

NAME _____

ADDRESS _____

CITY _____

STATE _____ ZIP NO. _____

____ Payment enclosed ____ I have an account at your store

Add sales tax where applicable

A Revell Publication